MW00438892

THE APE-SLAYER AND OTHER SNAPSHOTS

To Dear Day Smith
My friend

Bill Henry

THE APE-SLAYER AND OTHER SNAPSHOTS

A Collection of Random Writings

Bill Shipp

Mercer University Press
Macon, Georgia
1997

0-86554-571-5

The paper used in this publication meets the minimum requirements of
American National Standard for Permanence of Paper for Printed
Library Materials ANSI Z39.48–1984.

Jacket photograph by Ken Hawkins

Jacket design by Jim Burt

Library of Congress Cataloging-in-Publication Data
is available from the Library of Congress

TABLE OF CONTENTS

To my loving wife, Reny,
for her understanding and inspiration

In addition, I wish to thank my friends George Berry, Tom Brown, and Hal Gulliver for their often sound advice on this project; and my assistant, Joyce Manson, for organizing the material.

Introduction

Bill Shipp has been far and away the best political reporter in Georgia, and easily one of the best in the country, for more than two decades.

"There's an old country saying I've always loved. 'If you can't run with the big dogs, stay on the porch.' My friend Bill Shipp has always run with the big dogs. More than a few politicians—politicians bitten by his reporting—can testify," quoth Gene Tharpe, still laboring in the vineyards at the Atlanta newspapers, where he and I and Shipp once worked together on *The Atlanta Constitution* editorial board.

"His wife and family may disagree, but Bill—although friendly enough most of the time—was sometimes not a lovable fellow," adds Tharpe.

Tharpe has this annoying habit of saying things more pithily and accurately than I can, and I want him to know that I resent it. Happily, while Shipp is not always lovable, he is always a fine and perceptive writer, as this collection of columns and articles demonstrates over and over again.

Shipp sees the fun in politics, but he is also sometimes almost eerily prophetic.

Try this one, on the present speaker of the U.S. House:

"The next great Georgian could be a member of the GOP, a one-time gadfly college professor from Carrollton. ... Just think of it, there would be The Newt as our point man on the national scene. He would be there to take issue with the president on how to reinvigorate the economy. He would never see a war he didn't like or a treaty he did. He would denounce constantly the declining Democrats. ... Every time we flicked on C-SPAN, there would be Newt."

Fairly accurate, right?

Yet consider the date of this particular Shipp writing. It was in May 1991, when Newt still represented the old 6th District south of Atlanta and Congressman Bob Michel of Illinois was still the Republican minority leader. It was written fully three and one-half years before the 1994 elections swept the Republicans into the majority in the U.S. House and made Newt speaker of the House.

Almost eerie, I say.

Shipp plays fair in this collection by also including predictions that did not turn out to be quite so accurate. For example, at about the same time he predicted Our Man Newt would be on C-SPAN every day, he also wrote of then-President George Bush having "swept Georgia and the rest of the South against the Democratic ticket in the presidential election of 1988. He figures to do the same in 1992."

Now Bush and Shipp may have figured it that way; Bill Clinton did not. Ah, yes, Shipp, do you remember Bill Clinton? He was the presidential candidate whose campaign was faltering in early 1992. "He's just like a deer running through the woods," you said. "A hunter shoots him through the heart, but the deer doesn't feel it yet. He'll run for another hundred yards, then he'll drop like a rock." Some rock. That particular deer kept on running through the woods as far as the White House in 1992 and again in 1996, only the sixth president in more than a century to win two presidential elections. Can't win 'em all, ol' Shipp.

There are fine personal family reflections here, too, in the great Southern writing tradition, and one of the best is about the day Reny Shipp gave up her European roots and took the oath to become an American citizen. They had been married for 25 years at this point, and Reny, no doubt reluctantly, decided that this marriage might indeed last. Shipp's final words of advice to the Lady of the House: "Don't refer to yourself as a Yankee; register to vote and follow my advice at the polls. One other thing: We need to discuss the note you left this morning, the one that says I'll have to make my own breakfast from now on. You haven't become that American—have you, dear?"

Shipp has observed that the worry about doing a book such as this is that the "shelf life" of political columns may be slight.

Even the best political journalist only composes a snapshot of a single exact time. If the journalist is good enough, that snapshot reflects the landscape pretty well, and yet it may have all changed by the next election. But it is also true that the political situation at a precise time and place can be important.

Politics doesn't matter much to some people. Or, better put, they think it does not.

The late Helen Bullard, Atlanta's political adviser extraordinaire, said that she became absorbed with politics because something suddenly sank in on her one day. It was because of politics that Adolf Hitler ruled Germany and ruined much of Europe, murdering and torturing millions of Jews and non-Jews alike. That was politics, she said: a result of the legal election Hitler won in Germany in the early 1930s. Americans made a political choice in the early 1930s also. We elected Franklin D. Roosevelt president, a man who proved to be an honorable and heroic leader in both peace and war.

Were Germans so evil, Americans so smart, in the early 1930s? I tend to doubt that. There were probably, in proportion to population, fully as many good and decent Germans as there were good and decent Americans. But political decisions of that time led Germany along a terrible, immoral, barbarous, and evil path.

Politics does matter.

Gene Tharpe observes that when he first joined *The Atlanta Constitution* in the late 1960s, there were already "newspaper legends" on the scene, among them Jack Tarver and Celestine Sibley and Harold Martin. "Bill Shipp was building into one," says Tharpe. "He always was strong-willed. But for those of us who love the game, Bill Shipp was—and remains—the classic newspaperman."

— Hal Gulliver

SECTION I

PERSONALS

My American Wife

Syndicated column—February 11, 1982

This was not an ordinary week in our household. After 25 years, the Lady of the House made it official: She's decided to stay. She became an American citizen.

Standing in a spacious and somber courtroom on the 22nd floor of the Russell Federal Building, the Lady stood along with 69 other "green card aliens" and with a brief oath was miraculously transformed into a fellow American.

"I hereby declare, on oath, that I absolutely and entirely renounce and abjure all allegiance and fidelity to any foreign prince, potentate, state or sovereignty of whom or which I have heretofore been a subject or citizen," swore the applicants for citizenship in unison.

It was mostly an impressive ceremony. There was the oath of citizenship and the pledge to the flag; U.S. District Court Judge Frank Hooper, age 84, presided over the affair and signed the official order allowing my wife and her co-neophytes into the American club.

The new Americans were a mixed lot—a handful of German women (like the wife), several Russians, Vietnamese, Koreans, Indians, Scandinavians, and so on. Twenty-three nationalities in all were left behind.

Professions ranged from physician to shopkeeper to mechanic. This year in Atlanta, about 1,000 new Americans will step out into the world from the Russell Building, clutching their certificates of naturalization.

Those of us who are Americans by accident of birth ought to attend one of these ceremonies.

Not only do the rites remind us of our duties and our responsibilities, but they tell us why we are different and better than anyone else: We are free.

During the ceremony, the new citizens were reminded of their rights here. They were told of their freedoms under the Bill of Rights.

Then a young attorney reminded them of something most of us take for granted: As citizens, they could live where they pleased and move across state lines without government permission.

3

Watching the ceremony reminded one of something else: The face of the nation is changing. Less than half those who took the oath were European.

A few years ago, such a group would have been 75 percent European with only a sprinkling of Orientals and other ethnic groups and nationalities.

Since its inception, the face of this country has always changed as new waves of emigres sailed in from every shore. And perhaps it is that constant change in the mixture of the American blood which keeps us ahead of the pack ... and on top.

One thing must remain constant, however, and that is our language. The Immigration and Naturalization office here is fortunate in having one Terry Bird, 35, as its examining official. He is a stickler for seeing to it that would-be Americans can speak—and write—English. If they cannot, Bird sends them away and tells them to study up and re-apply in six months or a year.

Diversity in origin is important to the history and future of the United States. Being a nation of a single official language is just as important.

But enough of this. This started out as a congratulations to the Lady of the House for finally agreeing to renounce and abjure all allegiances and fidelity to Hapsburgs and their successors.

A couple of final words of advice, my Lady: Don't refer to yourself as a Yankee; register to vote and follow my advice at the polls.

One other thing: We need to discuss the note you left this morning, the one that says I'll have to make my own breakfast from now on. You haven't become that American—have you, dear?

This is so outdated and politically incorrect now that I cannot believe I wrote it. A nation with a single official language? Preposterous!

The Birth of Renewed Hope

The Atlanta Journal-Constitution — June 5, 1985

When I stepped up to the attractive receptionist at Northside Hospital and asked for my daughter Edie's room, she looked at me and said without smiling, "You must be the grandfather."

Grandfather?!!? Not me, babe. You've got the wrong guy. Why don't they teach those people a little tact? She could have said simply: "Are you related to the new parents?" or perhaps even, "You must be Baby Miles' uncle."

But, no, she laid it out there. The cold, harsh truth. No sugar coating. I am a grandpa. No more "Billy Boy." It'll be "Grandfather William" for the rest of the trip.

When I got up the day before Katie arrived in this old world, I looked into the mirror and saw a 51-year-young man. A few gray hairs here and there. A line or two under the eyes and across the forehead. A little overweight, perhaps. But an interesting-looking guy, one of the true sex symbols of American journalism. Sort of a younger and larger Paul Newman.

The lady at Northside shattered the illusion. Sex symbol of journalism, huh? If you are determined to flatter yourself, try "grand old man" for a better fit. And if you want to think of yourself as an actor, forget Paul Newman; think of John Houseman.

Look back into the mirror and what do you see now? A fat old guy with hair that has almost turned white. You're lucky you've still got hair. That may go soon, along with a couple of other things. You're not 51 years young either, sport. You'll be 52 years old in August, and you don't look a day over 65.

Take away the mirror. There must be a more joyous part to becoming a grandparent for the first time than being greeted by a medical receptionist who amputates your youth without benefit of anesthesia.

And there is. Just looking at this tiny new human being makes one feel a surge of renewed hope. The world, with all its miseries, doesn't seem so bad after all. But more than joy, one feels a sense of wonder. What kind of world will this child grow up in? Will she reach adulthood in a society dedicated to peace and progress? Or will her generation be the first to see wholesale nuclear destruction?

Will she see an end to worldwide hunger? Or will continuing overpopulation in parts of the world bring more famine and war?

Baby Kathryn has entered a world that is beset with problems. We are at peace, but sometimes we seem obsessed by the means of making war. We live in a prosperous time and place, but our fragile economy could easily unravel.

Despite all this, the outlook for Kathryn is good. She has arrived in the midst of an explosion of knowledge and enlightenment. The amount of information available to her seems limitless.

She has been born at a time when medical science is making unparalleled strides in eradicating whole categories of disease. Labor-saving devices will free up her generation from menial drudgery so that she may pursue more productive tasks.

Her gramps' vanity may have been bruised. But his pride in this brand-new addition to the family is as big as a mountain. And his hope for her future has given him a renewed sense of optimism for a better day.

So welcome to the world, Katie. It's a scary place in many ways. But it also can be beautiful. At least that's the way I hope it turns out for you.

Getting old, older, & oldest.

Fog on a Winter Morning

The Atlanta Journal-Constitution, 1985

At 5:00 A.M., I looked out an upstairs window into the fog that caressed the ground and shrouded the trees in back of the house.

My mind wandered backward in time. It was another foggy morning, just like this one. It was November 28, the Saturday after Thanksgiving 1982. And it wasn't five o'clock; it was about four. The phone was ringing. Ringing. Ringing.

"Hello."

"This is Officer [I don't remember his name] of the Cobb County police. Are you related to Ernie Shipp?"

"I'm his father."

"He has been in an accident."

"How serious is it?"

"I can't tell you over the phone. Come to the emergency room at Kennestone Hospital."

"I'll be right there."

I knew immediately that Ernie was dead. I did not tell Reny, my wife. I told her he had had a little trouble, and I would call her as soon as I learned the details. I told her not to worry. It was too late for that anyhow.

We lived near Powder Springs at the time. The 15-minute drive to the hospital in Marietta seemed to last a lifetime. But I almost enjoyed it. The fog was thick, and the streets were empty. I knew the peace and solitude would be the last I would have for a long time.

When I reached the hospital, I asked the nurse about my son. She escorted me to a private sitting room where a man and woman, about my age, were crying. Then she told me what I had expected to hear. She said, "Ernie was killed in a car wreck, along with two other boys."

They weren't boys; they were men, I almost said. But that was silly. She said she wanted me to identify the body. She led me to another room in which the corpses of three young men, covered with sheets, were stretched out on tables. I heard myself crying and felt tears stream down my face. She pulled back the sheet from Ernie's face. There he was, sleeping and bloody and finally at peace with himself.

I don't remember exactly what happened next. I called home and started to tell Reny what had happened. But I couldn't. I told her to put

7

our daughter Michelle on the phone. I told Michelle simply: "Ernie is dead." She screamed. At that moment, I realized how stupid I had been. I should have told them face to face. I needed to get home quickly. I turned and became confused and lost in the hospital corridors. I sheepishly asked someone to direct me out.

I don't even remember the drive home or exactly what happened next. There was a lot of running around and phone calls about getting the body released to the funeral home. Then there was the funeral, and the great crowd of mourners who came to the chapel and to the house. And suddenly it was empty. We, my wife and I, hit bottom and didn't bounce.

I have written twice before about Ernie's death, believing that the catharsis might ease the pain. The last time I wrote of him was Christmas 1984. I said everything is all right now: The hurt is mostly healed. I lied.

I have tried everything to blur the memories and muffle the screaming inside my head. Since his death, I have traveled on assignments to Asia, Europe and Africa. I have been all over the country, covering political campaigns, court hearings and sundry other irrelevant topics. The people at the newspaper, particularly the editor, Jim Minter, seemed to understand that I needed to be occupied. I have bought a new home and new furniture and new cars. I have changed my lifestyle. I have immersed myself in work.

At Ernie's funeral, someone told me that a tragedy of this magnitude would bring my wife and me closer together than ever. Wrong. We drifted apart for a time, suffering in isolation and somehow blaming each other for his death, though only God knows why. He was a passenger in a speeding car that struck a utility pole. No matter what we had or had not done for him in life, he would still have died at that time and that place.

But grief is a selfish emotion for us. We found it difficult, at least for a while, to share with each other, let alone with anyone else.

Just when I think the hurt is subsiding, something brings it all back. Like the fog on a winter morning, three years after his death.

With Love, Grandpa

The Atlanta Journal-Constitution — December 25, 1985

Dear Katie and Jessica:

Welcome to your first Christmas, granddaughters. You're too young for this special time to have much meaning this year. But wait 'til next year and the year after that. Your eyes will glow with excitement, and the suspense will seem unbearable as you wonder what gifts will miraculously appear under the Christmas tree.

I hope your parents teach you early that Christmas is more than material gifts, that the best gifts are not in shiny packages. It ought to be a time when all Christendom stops and takes stock. Are we even close to living up to any of the tenets of the Preacher of Peace whose birth we celebrate?

I wonder how He would react today, 2,000 years after the first Christmas, to a world that includes building and perfecting devices to slaughter whole populations, terrorism in the name of religion, and epidemic starvation.

I also wonder, Katie and Jessica, if Christmas and the world in which we live will change as much in the next half century as it has in the past 50-plus years since I saw my first Christmas tree.

My first Christmas came in the year Franklin Roosevelt was sworn in as 32nd president of the United States. His presidency would change our entire notion about the role of government in relieving human suffering and deprivation.

In that same year, 1933, Adolf Hitler became chancellor of Germany, an event that would spread death, destruction, and dislocation throughout the world and ultimately change our lives forever, even in then-rural Cobb County, Georgia.

It also would give you a grandmother who speaks Southern with a Czech accent.

Those first Christmases, as I grew up, had a fascinating sameness about them. The season would invariably begin in early December when my dad decided it was time to go to the Giles farm near Acworth to get a Christmas tree. He would carry along an ax to cut the tree and a shotgun to shoot mistletoe out of the same stand of oaks that played host to it year after year.

(One of the small rites of manhood occurred in my 9th or 10th December when "Rusty" handed me the shotgun to bring down the mistletoe.)

Occasionally during Christmastime, my grandfather, Papa Shipp, would take me with him on the streetcar from the town square in Marietta to the state Capitol, where he worked, to see the decorations in far-away Atlanta.

The lights and Great Tree were dazzling, but the real thrill was the ride on the electric streetcar.

On Christmas Eve, I would wake in the middle of the night, thinking I heard sounds outside, sounds, I was certain, of a fat man in a red suit, driving a sleigh over red clay.

On Christmas morning, I would leap from bed and race into the living room to see what bright new toys had been left for me. (If you grew up in the South in the Depression, I suppose you are expected to describe the bleakness and austerity of Christmas time. It wasn't that way at our house. Both my parents worked, and they splurged on their only child at Christmas.)

Cowboy suits, cap pistols, and electric trains that looked like steam locomotives were the centerpieces of the toy collection. Books, bicycles, and skates came later. In the 1940s, Army helmets, toy machine guns and model fighter planes replaced the cowboy gear, six-guns, and trains.

We would spend Christmas Day at my grandparents' with their great extended family. I am certain I had at least two dozen cousins who showed up on that day to enjoy a magnificent feast of succulent meats and steaming vegetables, nearly all home-grown.

When the 1940s came, some of the men disappeared from the traditional Christmas gathering. They had gone to war. All my relatives, save one distant cousin shot down over Germany, returned.

Bell Aircraft Corp. built the "bummer plant" just outside Marietta. That once-sleepy town seemed to explode overnight with activity. Farmers left their plows to make airplanes. Housewives and store clerks moved to the assembly line. The war not only ended the Depression in Cobb County; it erased a simple, rural lifestyle that had much to recommend it.

(Cumberland Mall and the zillion cars around it sit where my dad and I once ran hounds and hunted birds and rabbits.)

Aw, your grandpa is rambling. This was supposed to be a piece of advice for you on Christmas. So here it is: When you are 5 or 6 years old, some young man of similar age, seeking to impress you, will confide he has discovered there is no Santa Claus. He is lying. Have nothing more to do with this rogue.

10

Meanwhile, have a merry Christmas, little girls. There is indeed a Santa Claus. Among the gifts he bears is hope for a better world for you and yours.

On May 12, 1988, Katie's sister, Hillary, was born. The kids have grown older, and so I have I. But this piece speaks for itself, about some values, memories, and people I still hold dear.

Breakfast with Reny

Atlanta Magazine — February 1990

Reny could go home again. The Communist regime in Czechoslovakia had fallen. The barbed-wire fences on the border had been destroyed. A new "Prague spring" was on the way. The face of Europe changed at the end of the 1980s at nearly the same lightning speed Hitler had changed it in the 1930s and '40s. Except this time it was a freedom blitz. The Cold War was finished. World War II was all but forgotten. Germany could soon unify. After 33 years in this country, Reny, 56, was free to return to where she lived as a child.

The cruel memories might disappear once she saw the old places again. A trip back might do us both good. We talked about it on a cold Sunday morning. We spoke quietly over coffee in a house in a subdivision in Cobb County where Reny, once a frightened little girl driven at gunpoint from her home in Europe, now lives as a gracefully aging grandmother.

This is the essence of that conversation (and several earlier ones) between this American husband and his Czech-born wife:

HE: You ought to go back. We'll both go. I've always wanted to visit Prague. We'll go in April or May.

SHE: I don't want to go. There's no one left. My oldest sister is dead. She was the only one we left behind. What would I do there?

HE: We could visit Prague, then go up near the Polish border to Frydek-Mistek, where you grew up.

SHE: Why would I want to go there?

HE: Don't you want to see where you lived when you were a little girl?

SHE: Why? Do I want to see where they threw my father into a concentration camp, where the Czechs spat on him? Where six Russians raped a 13-year-old girl and she cut her wrists? Where they raped an 80-year-old woman across the street? Where they took everything we had and made us get into cattle cars and threw us out of the country?

HE: It wasn't all bad. We've talked about that before. You lived pretty well before the war.

SHE: Yes. I was very young then. I don't remember much about it. My father ran a tailor shop, and my mother had a little milk-and-cheese business on the side. We were Czechs, but we were also Germans. My mother won an Iron Cross—for having so many children (eight). My father was a member of something called the SA, a German political group. I've told you all about that.

HE: Prague is a beautiful city. Wouldn't you like to see it again?

SHE: I was 12 years old the last time I was in Prague. I had been in a Hitler Youth camp. The war suddenly ended, or at least it ended for us. The camp was dissolved, and we were left to go wherever the wind blew us. My girlfriend and I wanted desperately to get home. She was very ill and running a high fever. We got on a train in Prague and started home. Everyone else was going in the opposite direction. They were trying to get away from the Russians. It was chaos. Maybe you're right. Prague is a wonderful city. I don't remember it that way. My girlfriend died shortly after we got back to Frydek. Then the Russians came.

HE: That was so long ago. Wouldn't you like to learn firsthand how the Czechs live now?

SHE: No. I know them too well. I will never forget how they treated us before we left. The Czechs would not let us go out in the street. They took our belongings. They cursed us. They made all the Germans wear yellow armbands with black lettering that said: "We thank you, our fuhrer." (Do you know why they made the Germans wear yellow and black armbands? Because the Germans made the Jews wear yellow stars with black letters.)

The headmaster at the school was forced to sweep the streets. Even the Czechs who had pretended to be our friends during the German times mistreated us. My mother had tried to help them with food and clothing. When the Russians and Czech partisans took control, the Czechs turned into animals for a time. My own sister turned out to be not so very nice. She was a Communist, of course. Do you think what is happening now will change the character of the people? Eastern Europeans thrive on hate and prejudice. You will see.

HE: OK. Forget Prague. Let's go to Germany. You've never wanted to go back. Now the whole atmosphere has changed. We could go back to Heidelberg where we met—and be romantic again.

SHE: Let me tell you about Germany. We were Germans in Czechoslovakia. And we were considered gypsies in Germany. We were thrown out of Czechoslovakia because we were Germans and took the Germans' side in the war. Then when we came to Germany—to Sandhausen just outside Heidelberg—in 1946, the Germans despised us. We were crowding them. There were so many refugees pouring in from all over Eastern Europe. The Germans had to give up some of

13

their living quarters for us. They resented us. They forgot that we took much of the punishment that they deserved.

HE: Yes, but we're talking about 45 years ago. Haven't you been keeping up with all that's happening now? Germany will soon be one nation again.

SHE: Just wait. When the euphoria about rejoining East Germany subsides, you will see what happens. The West Germans will begin to resent them just as they resented us. And for the same reasons. They will crowd them and take their jobs and cause trouble.

HE: If I had not been married to you for lo these many years, I might think you were a bitter old woman.

SHE: You are wrong as usual. I am simply realistic. No one has bothered to think very deeply about what this upheaval in Europe means in the long term. The television commentators want to say it means an end to communism. Communism is not what this was about. The revolution came because the East Europeans tired of not having cars and homes and television sets and not even enough toilet paper. For the most part, they don't care whether the government is communist or democratic or even fascist. You have to understand that.

HE: We could go to Heidelberg again. Don't you remember how that was? The Americans weren't so bad, now were they?

SHE (giggling): I remember how the Americans were all right.

HE: Never mind that. I'm trying to write a piece on the changes in Eastern Europe, and I want you to go back there with me.

SHE: Let me tell you about the Americans. The first Americans I ever saw were in Czechoslovakia. They were two airplane pilots. They had just bombed our town, and they were shot down. Their plane crashed in a field near the river. They were taken prisoner by the SS, who had headquarters near our house. All my friends and I ran to the window to watch the Americans when they came out of the SS headquarters. The Germans brought them out after a while. The Americans were laughing. The Germans gave them cigarettes, then took their wristwatches and drove them away. ...

When we got off the freight train in Germany at the first refugee camp, I saw my first American blacks. My eyes got as big as saucers. Until then, I thought of them as being sort of fabled characters. The black GIs gave us candy and had fun with us kids. They could tell we thought we were in a storybook-land and were amazed at seeing these black-skinned people.

HE: Look, I've been back to Europe a half-dozen times since we were married. And you've never wanted to go back. Now things have changed.

SHE: What has changed? Nothing has changed. The French still hate the Germans; the Germans still hate the Poles; the Czechs still hate the Slovaks. Everybody hates the Americans and the Russians.

HE: I don't believe I am hearing this. You are more enlightened than that. Just watch television. Didn't you see the Berlin Wall come down and Dubcek being hailed as a hero in Prague? Aren't you happy about that? Don't you wish these people well?

SHE: Of course I do. But I have lost nothing in Eastern Europe. My life is here. I am no more a European now than you are. I am an American. Look at our children and grandchildren, if you doubt I am an American—and a Southerner. Who bought that Civil War print for our anniversary? Who told that New York newspaper publisher that I was a Georgian? He thought I meant Soviet Georgia. I said, "No, I am from Atlanta." And he said, "I didn't know Georgia crackers had such funny accents."

HE: We're getting off the subject. We ought to go back to Europe. Just as tourists, not as journalists or former expellees or anything like that. Just as gawking American tourists. Now that wouldn't be so bad, would it?

SHE: Maybe you're right. We could go to that little place in Heidelberg where we met. ...

HE: Where I picked you up. ...

SHE: You did not pick me up. I simply stole your heart.

HE: And my money. ... (Laughter) I want to write about what's happening in Eastern Europe through the eyes of someone who has lived there and would like to go back.

SHE: OK. But let's wait. Let the turmoil settle down. I don't care to watch any more upheavals. You may like riots and demonstrations. I saw enough of those a long time ago.

HE: What do you think is finally going to happen?

SHE: How the hell should I know? You're the pundit in the house. My guess is, the Americans and the Russians will finally pull out all their soldiers. The Germans will get together and get arrogant again. The Americans will become isolationist again. The French and the British will get nervous again. The whole thing will start all over. ...

Let's have breakfast. I want to go shopping.

Remembering Three Decades of Change

Syndicated column—May 6, 1992

Last week's scenes of mob violence in Los Angeles and Atlanta sent my memory reeling back in time 30 years.

It is 1962—a year in some ways much like 1992, and in others, a year that seems from another century and another place. There are major riots and racial disturbances. On a university campus, armed students fire on federal officers, set fires, overturn cars and destroy other property. At least three persons are killed, scores injured.

The mob is white. The place: Ole Miss, Oxford, Miss. The federal government has ordered the first black student, James Meredith, admitted to the University of Mississippi.

In Georgia, 1962, Dr. Martin Luther King Jr. leads mostly nonviolent demonstrations against segregation in Albany. He is jailed. A young assistant, Andrew Young, negotiates with white leaders for his release and for an end to racially separate public accommodations.

In Atlanta, Ivan Allen Jr. presides as mayor. Racial moderation is the watchword. Don't let Atlanta become another Birmingham or Little Rock. So command the white leaders of the community. Their order is obeyed.

Atlanta is about to take off economically. Big-league sports will settle in the capital city. New skyscrapers will shortly spring up. The freeways are packed. So is the airport. Business has never been better.

In Washington, John F. Kennedy presides over Camelot. If he has flaws, we don't notice. He meets the Soviets eyeball to eyeball in the October Cuban missile crisis. The Soviets flinch. American military aid to South Vietnam escalates.

I was a 28-year-old reporter that year. It was an exciting time to be alive. I covered the flight of John Glenn in a tiny Project Mercury capsule, the first American astronaut to orbit the Earth. I reported first-hand the violence at Ole Miss and Albany and Birmingham. Despite the racial turmoil, it was a time of optimism. And I was bulletproof. At least I believed I was.

By the end of that decade, Kennedy and King would be assassinated. President Lyndon Johnson would have lost two wars: the military one in Vietnam and the social one against domestic poverty.

16

Atlanta, still prospering, had become a city in transition. Soon, black political leaders would control City Hall and Fulton County government.

Affirmative-action programs would replace equal-opportunity edicts. Set-asides would become automatic. Millions of tax dollars, state and federal, were poured into programs to uplift minorities.

A moderate Georgia governor, Jimmy Carter, would become president by forging a coalition of white and black Democrats. He had begun his statewide political career in 1962 as a candidate for the state Senate.

Last week as I stood at the northwest corner of the Capitol lawn and listened to the crackle of a police radio, my heart speeded up. I was ready again to cover another conflict. Platoons of specially trained corrections officers and state rangers, outfitted in riot gear, lined up two abreast to prepare for a confrontation with rioters.

They looked much like the squadrons of young guardsmen and federal marshals ready to engage the mobs in Oxford, Miss., three decades ago.

In 1962, a liberal press complained rightly about racial injustice. In 1992, the same complaints fill the air, along with rocks and bottles.

As in 1962, millions of blacks are still mired in poverty. Never mind the billions of dollars wasted in the war on poverty or the volumes of laws guaranteeing equal rights, affirmative action and political influence. They haven't worked.

Voices espousing racial integration fell silent long ago. Dr. King's vision of a racially integrated America, a land in which color doesn't count, never materialized. Racial separatists are in now. Nonviolence has become passé.

For a moment last week, I considered wandering off into the inner city to check out the new mob, to watch again as thugs and lawmen collided. Then I had second thoughts and decided instead to head for the safety of home. One thing had changed since 1962: I no longer believe I am bulletproof.

17

Another View of 'Official English'

Syndicated column—February 8, 1995

"What do you mean, 'They don't want to learn English'? That is nonsense. It is the least that should be required of them. They ought to thank the stars that they have been allowed to stay in this country. If they don't want to learn English, let them go back where they came from."

These may sound like sentiments of a member of the Daughters of the American Revolution or one of the original descendants of the Mayflower voyagers. Or certainly of a diehard Anglophilic xenophobe.

Sorry, none of the above. Such harsh words flow from the lips of one Frau Renate Friedericke Reineltova Shipp, the mother of my children, the co-head of our household, a yellow-dog Democrat and a lady with an accent so pronounced, even after these 38 years, that one might believe she just stepped off the plane.

She has learned of the public outcry at the state Capitol against the attempt to promote English as our authorized language. And she is upset at the protesters. English is her third or perhaps fourth language. She was born in Czechoslovakia to Czech- and German-speaking parents. In school in Germany, she chose to learn Russian, instead of English, as her other language. She did not take up English until she was well into her 20s and came to this country in the 1950s.

She recalls being chastised by an Atlanta physician when she failed to comprehend his instructions, given in English, during her first pregnancy. "If you want to stay here, learn the language," he admonished. "He was right. I learned English," she says.

Frau Shipp is baffled by the current controversy over an innocuous bill in the Georgia Legislature making English the standard language of state government. The measure does not require that English be spoken or understood. It simply says state government documents must be published in English and will not necessarily be published in other languages.

Senator Mike Crotts, R-Conyers, introduced the "English bill" last year, and it failed. It is likely to be killed again this year.

Black activists are opposed to the bill because, they contend, it promotes discrimination. Their stance is somewhat puzzling because (1) most of them were born into English-speaking families, and (2) the greatest economic rivals to native blacks are newly arrived Hispanics, held back mostly by lack of skill in English.

Hispanic organizations are leading the charge to void the bill, because they say it harms non-English-speaking Latino immigrants.

Precisely what's going on here is not clear. This is not a legislative initiative from the lunatic right or a radical resolution that would drastically alter how we live and think. The official business of Georgia is now conducted in English. There has been growing pressure in this state and others to force the use of other languages, principally Spanish, in carrying out official duties.

Making the state and nation multilingual is a bad idea. There is ample precedent. Canada will never be a major international power because it is torn between English- and French-speakers.

Belgium is a European backwater, divided by French and Flemish.

Other nations recognize the importance of protecting their language. France established a national commission to protect French. In that nation, it is a crime to use many foreign words, including English ones, in advertising and certain commercial transactions. In Germany, one cannot get a driver's license or participate in many other activities without being able to read and write German.

(To avoid the appearance of yielding to the supremacy of either's language, the French and Germans conduct much of the official dialogue between their two nations in English.)

Spanish is the official language of Mexico, whence comes the flood of immigrants demanding we not abuse them by declaring English is our authorized tongue.

A nation and its culture survive when its people are secured from domestic danger, the integrity of its borders is maintained, and its common language is protected. Our government has already failed in two of those missions, and it doesn't seem to have much stomach for trying to carry out the third.

Mike Crotts doesn't defend his bill as anything as grand as an attempt to preserve our customs and traditions. He claims only that it would save taxpayers money by reducing the number of multilingual documents required of state agencies.

Yet, he is targeted as a bigot and a chauvinist crank for proposing such a law.

Frau Shipp wonders what has happened to this country since she came here nearly 40 years ago and a doctor advised her to learn English if she intended to stay.

A watered-down version of the Official English bill finally passed the Legislature and was signed into law by Gov. Miller.

The Difference a Decade Makes

Georgia Trend – September 1995

My work day in 1995: At 5:30 A.M., I walk 20 steps from my bedroom to my office, adjust my computer, dial up the AP, *The New York Times*, *The Washington Post* and *The Atlanta Journal-Constitution*. I pour a cup of coffee and scan the headlines on the screen. I download the stories that interest me.

A few minutes later, I check my e-mail and find messages and correspondents' stories for my newsletter or notes from associates about the day's activities. By 6:30 A.M., I begin writing.

By 7:30 A.M., my CEO/editor/office manager, Joyce Manson, who lives across the street, has arrived at corporate headquarters for my publishing empire, Word Merchants Inc., a little room in my basement. I transmit the results of my pre-dawn labors to her computer. She edits the material and disseminates it to newspapers, an on-line service, this magazine or prepares it for a commercial printer who produces our newsletter, *Bill Shipp's Georgia*. My home-delivered newspapers are still in the driveway. I may get to them later.

It is now time to shave and have breakfast. Then I will head for the Capitol to talk to politicians or do whatever else is on the day's agenda. The morning rush hour is over.

My work day in 1985: At 6:30 A.M., I roll out of bed, put on a robe, get the papers from the driveway (if they have been delivered), take a shower and shave.

I slip into a dark suit, wing tips, a starched white shirt, and tie. I scan the papers quickly and turn on the TV for a bit of "Good Morning America."

It is 8:00 A.M. when I get into the car and head 27 miles south to the office at *The Atlanta Journal-Constitution*. If there are no traffic problems, I will be there in 45 minutes. It usually takes more than an hour.

At the office, I have a cup of coffee, thumb through a few other papers, make a couple of phone calls, chat with colleagues, and prepare for the daily 11 o'clock editorial meeting.

The meeting usually lasts until 11:30. Then it is time to start working on the day's assignments—except it is nearly noon and lunchtime. ...

Thinking back, I am startled by the contrast in my work routine over the past decade.

Of course, my circumstances have changed. In 1985, I was a small cog—an editor and writer—in a great downtown Atlanta corporation, Cox Enterprises Inc.

In 1995, I own a tiny publishing business and information service.

But more has changed than my personal situation. In 10 years, a desktop computer attached to a phone line has turned my world of work—and the media—upside down. The revolution has just begun. By 2005, we will look back on 1995—and certainly 1985—as part of the horse-and-buggy era of communications.

Thousands of commuters, who braved rush-hour traffic day after day, have decided the home office is a better, more productive place to work.

Bosses have changed, too. The corporate papa is disappearing.

When I returned from the Army in 1956, my father advised: "Get a job with a big company and stay there. If you work hard and keep your nose clean, they will take care of you." It worked for Dad. He retired from Southern Bell after 40 years, and the company took care of him.

I stayed with Cox for the better part of three decades, and the firm has not been unkind since I resigned.

But those days of long-term corporate monogamy are about over. Since I left Cox in 1987, I have been affiliated with four other companies besides my own.

No more dramatic changes have occurred than in the industry of which I am a part—the business of collecting and disseminating information.

In 1985, Gene Patterson, who had been a bright and articulate editor of *The Atlanta Constitution* during the 1950s and '60s, was running the newspapers in St. Petersburg, Fla. He saw Atlanta and Georgia as an inviting home for a new magazine, *Georgia Trend.*

Several other magazines were prospering in Atlanta. Economic times had never been better than they were in the mid-'80s. *The Atlanta Journal-Constitution* was setting circulation records, though the afternoon *Journal* had begun to slip.

The New York Times was eyeing the region to start a venture of its own, possibly in competition with the established newspapers. American Express, with executive ties to Atlanta, was about to get more involved in media.

21

All-news radio was the rage, though Rush Limbaugh was yet to be heard from. The big-three TV networks, ABC, CBS, and NBC, dominated the television scene through their outlets at Channels 2, 5, and 11. CBS was considered the best, if not "most watched" news network. No one had heard of Fox or ever considered that pro football might one day move to a "minor channel." The UHF channels were shrugged off. On-line information services were in their infancy.

Southern Bell was the only local telephone game in town, though several other companies operated elsewhere in the state.

In 1986, the media boat in Atlanta began to rock frantically.

Cox decided it was ready for Broadway with its Atlanta dailies. It brought in Bill Kovach, a well-meaning, Washington-based *New York Times* bureau chief, to replace Georgia native Jim Minter as editor of the *Journal-Constitution*. Kovach would squeeze out many of the newspapers' old hands (including this one), who had been identified with the era of publisher Ralph McGill and former Cox president Jack Tarver.

Kovach also would make over the paper in the style of a *New York Times*, finally winning a Pulitzer Prize for a series on bank lending practices. The editorial staffs at the newspapers were expanded to the size of *The Washington Post's*.

Kovach bucked the trend toward brightness and brevity. He lasted until just before the elections of 1988, when Cox management decided to accept his repeatedly offered resignation.

A few months later, the newspapers were morphed again—this time by a former Gannett editor, Ron Martin, who restyled them in the shape of *USA Today*. Short stories, color graphics, and plenty of pictures turned the *Constitution* and the *Journal* into a sort of MTV-version of newspapers.

High production costs began to take their toll. The Atlanta newspapers, which once prided themselves on statewide dominance, gradually withdrew into the metro region. They tried to reach out to the suburbs with special "Extras," but their hearts were in the declining central city. A business columnist who ventured outside the city limits once wrote a piece expressing astonishment at the growth she discovered in north Fulton and Cobb counties.

The New York Times bought out the venerable *Gwinnett Daily News* and made an unsuccessful bid on *The Marietta Daily Journal*. The *Times* intended to take the lucrative north-metro market from the *AJC*.

American Express acquired *Atlanta Magazine* and hired veteran newsman Lee Walburn from the *AJC* to run it. The credit card giant would turn Atlanta into a national model for city magazines—before deciding it was a costly luxury it could not sustain.

The exodus of the media newcomers began as suddenly as their arrival.

Cox turned full attention to driving *The New York Times* out of its market. The *Times* made a series of financial blunders here and in New York, and folded *The Gwinnett Daily News* and retreated to Manhattan.

American Express unloaded *Atlanta Magazine*. Grimes Publications bought *Georgia Trend* from *The St. Petersburg Times*, sold it to Williams Communications, then bought it back again. *Business Atlanta* went out of business, and its remains were purchased by *Georgia Trend*.

Though suburban newspapers and some magazines flourished, the bell had begun to toll for big-time paper journalism. The cost of newsprint went up and up and up—and is still going up. Afternoon newspapers, including the once-dominant *Atlanta Journal*, faded. Editions were canceled, and space for news reduced.

It doesn't take a futurist to figure out that the end of big-city newspapers as we know them is just over the next hill.

Ten years ago, I wore a tie and suit and worked 40 hours a week out of a corner office in a downtown high-rise. Today, I work 60 hours, mostly wearing a tattered bathrobe, out of an office next to my bedroom.

I am not alone. There are millions like me. Our lives and lifestyles will change even more in the coming years as we move into this digital world that holds the twin promises of expanded enlightenment and prolonged economic displacement.

Confessions of a White Male Gun Nut

Syndicated column — August 14, 1996

I am a white male, a born-again Christian, and a gun nut. That ought to put me squarely in the mainstream of the current Republican Party.

After all, more than 90 percent of the delegates to the Republican National Convention are white. Nearly 60 percent are male, and more than a third claim membership in an evangelical church. Over half favor lifting the ban on the sale of assault weapons.

That's where my profile as a true-believer Republican begins to unravel. Not all of us gun nuts are enthusiastic about letting every Tom, Dick, or Andre buy assault weapons.

Not all of us are dedicated to the goals of the National Rifle Association or own shares of gun-making corporations.

Some of us who are collectors and have long experience with firearms believe it is plain crazy to advocate the sale of assault weapons. The prohibition on sales should be broadened, not rescinded. Putting assault weapons back on store shelves and into the hands of would-be shootists has nothing to do with the constitutional right to bear arms.

It relates to gang warfare in our cities. Assault weapons pose a threat to our safety and the safety of our families.

The homicide rate in the city of Atlanta is spiraling. Atlanta experienced an average of one homicide a day during the Olympics. Its murder rate is running either 60 percent or 80 percent ahead of last year, depending on whose statistics you believe.

Handguns were involved in most of the killings. Take the lid off selling semi-automatic machine pistols and see what happens.

Atlanta is less safe than Sarajevo, Attorney General Mike Bowers said a few weeks before the Olympics began. Everyone gasped that the AG would dare be so critical of Atlanta on the eve of the Games. Turns out Bowers' assertion was an understatement. Sarajevo is a much safer city than Atlanta.

Yet, a Republican leader, Rep. Bob Barr, who lives at the rim of the state capital, is a captain of a national crusade to open up the sale of assault weapons. He also is adamantly opposed to putting identifying markers in explosives, or even studying the possibility.

If the feds had such ID available, they might now have indictments against the person or persons who set off the murderous nail-bomb in Centennial Park a couple of weeks ago.

Rep. Barr is a mainstream GOP congressman. He escaped opposition in the last Republican primary. The last time we checked, his Democratic opponent, former state Rep. Charlie Watts of Dallas, Ga., echoed most of Barr's sentiments in favor of the NRA's goals.

Then there's the religious part of being a proud Republican. That may let me out too. In the church of my youth, "tolerance" was considered a virtue. In today's realm of the Christian Coalition, "tolerance" borders on sin.

More than 50 percent of the Republican convention delegates favor severe restrictions on immigration, including denying public assistance and education to the children of illegal immigrants.

That seems sound enough. Without doubt, new immigrants strain our resources and change our culture in ways that are not always pleasant. A few generations back, Indian chiefs faced the same problems with us. And look what happened to them.

The anti-immigrant sentiment puts another hole in my newly discovered profile as a Republican. My bride of nearly 40 years escaped central Europe and came to this country because of a compassionate Republican of another era and his now-defunct Dwight Eisenhower Refugee Act, which waived quotas for certain destitute and persecuted groups.

The atmosphere gets a bit chilly in our house when there's even a hint of saying "amen" to the present Republican position of socking it to immigrants.

SECTION II

PERSONALITIES

The Ape-Slayer

Syndicated column—September 30, 1987

This is a police story. Or maybe a police-academy story. It is about Atlanta Patrolman Richard Hyde of Lawrenceville, who has decided after eight years he's not cut out to be a cop. He's too much the eager beaver. He's too impolitic to get along with City Hall. He's looking for a new career.

In his relatively short tenure, Hyde, at 28, has done about everything a policeman would ever think of doing—and some a policeman might never dare try. He has arrested big shots, wounded a robbery suspect (the wrong guy as it turned out), and even killed an ape gone berserk. He rescued four men from a burning building and won the Police Bureau's "Meritorious Award" badge for courage.

Now Hyde is facing disciplinary charges growing out of the Julian Bond affair. One of the accusations, filed against him by Atlanta Public Safety Commissioner George Napper, is that he reported the Julian Bond mess to the FBI.

"I thought I was doing my duty as a citizen," says Hyde. "I didn't know it was a crime to talk to the FBI." He played for the FBI a taped interview with Alice (Mrs. Julian) Bond after he became convinced the Atlanta police were not interested in pursuing her allegations of cocaine use among Atlanta's black elite.

This is not the first time Hyde has been in hot water with his superiors. Hyde admits he has been in the cop dog house almost from the day he entered the police academy.

"I should have seen the handwriting on the wall at the academy when an instructor asked my class, 'Who would arrest the mayor for drunk driving?' I was the only one who raised a hand. Since then, I've been a pariah."

Here are highlights of Hyde's career as described by Hyde:

—When he was assigned to the Atlanta airport, he arrested two men engaged in sodomy in a men's room. One suspect turned out to be an airline executive, the other a federal official. Hyde's superior suggested he forget the incident.

—On the night of the grand opening of the new Hartsfield Mid-Field Terminal, Hyde arrested a state senator on his way home from the

29

party for driving under the influence. He called two police supervisors to the arrest scene, and they quickly freed the senator.

— Next Hyde was transferred to southwest Atlanta where, he says, "I was putting a lot of people in jail for burglary and robbery." One night, Hyde spotted a long black sedan speeding through his area. He chased the car and finally pulled it over. He whipped out his pistol, only to find himself facing then-Deputy Police Chief Eldrin Bell.

— It was off to the motorcycle squad for Hyde. While cruising around the Capitol one day, he noticed nine cars parked illegally. He ordered them towed away. The nine vehicles were owned by state legislators.

— Hyde was sent to northeast Atlanta, where things are not usually quite so exciting. Except one night, he heard on his radio the description of a suspect in a nightclub robbery. He saw a man on the street fitting the description and ordered him to halt. When the fellow fled, Hyde shot and wounded him. He was the wrong man. He had fled because he was carrying a package of marijuana.

— Then there was the time Hyde was on his way home from work when he saw an old warehouse on fire. He raced inside the burning building and rescued four derelicts who were asleep. Chief Morris Redding presented him the Meritorious Award for courage.

— On another occasion, Hyde emptied his revolver into the chest of a rampaging chimpanzee who had escaped its owner and was running amok on Piedmont Avenue. "He maimed five people and threw a wrecker driver completely over a car before I shot him," Hyde says. The chimp's owner was distraught.

In his spare time, Hyde blew the whistle on two fellow officers for shaking down a nightclub owner; he went to Attorney General Mike Bowers to ask for an investigation of ticket-fixing in the Atlanta traffic court; he reported his supervisors for leaving their shifts early; he nailed an attorney for bribery.

At one point, Police Chief Morris Redding assigned Hyde to sit on a couch in his outer office "and not do anything—just sit there."

When the Julian Bond scandal erupted—and the charges were brought against Hyde for going to the FBI—he was sent back to southeast Atlanta, where he has been beaten by a man he tried to arrest and injured in a hit-and-run auto collision. Hyde believes he may have been set up in both incidents. He is now assigned to a desk job in police headquarters while he recovers from his injuries and awaits disposition of the charges against him.

"I've decided to quit. I want to make enough money to support my family and live a quiet life. But I've had enough of police work. It's just not worth it. You don't have to be poor and black to have civil rights. ..."

My rights are being violated. Anybody has a right to go to the FBI," says Hyde.

Hyde is 30 hours away from a college degree at Georgia State University. He earns $27,000 as a policeman and works at two other part-time jobs. He has a wife and one child and another on the way. He owns his home in Lawrenceville. He has a lot of energy.

Hyde could not stay away from law enforcement. In 1997, he was the state attorney general's lead investigator on a case that led to the arrest of two Medical College of Georgia faculty members and allegations they pocketed $10 million that should have gone to the University System for drug research.

A Soldier's Story

Atlanta Magazine—November 1988

On a rainy day in August 1956, I waved a temporary goodbye to a pretty little brunette standing on the platform of the Heidelberg Hauptbahnhof. I was on my way to the airport in Frankfurt, then on to New York. My military career was coming to a close. I felt great. I was leaving the Army with my body and soul not only intact but in better shape than when I signed up.

Three months later, I would be a civilian sitting on the rim of a newspaper copy desk in Atlanta. The brunette would be my wife. And we would live more or less happily ever after. Variations of that story have been played out a million times.

Many men did not leave military service in one piece. Max Cleland came home from the Army in a basket. He was lucky it wasn't a box. His body, if not his soul, was shredded by high explosives in Vietnam. He lost his legs and right arm. A hole had been blown in his psyche, but it healed. Some people said Max must be a lonely guy, all disfigured and crippled like that. But how could he be lonely? There is always somebody with him, pushing his wheelchair and helping him get in and out of it, even when he goes to the toilet.

Variations of that story have been played out thousands of times.

Cleland wasn't like a lot of Vietnam vets, though. He wasn't a whiner. By God, he had been a good soldier, and he was proud of it. So what if he'd been blown apart in 'Nam? He'd show them. He'd snap back. And he did.

He wrote an inspirational book, *Strong at the Broken Places*, about his experience. He was elected to the Georgia state Senate. He was Jimmy Carter's pal and the first person Carter officially received when Carter moved into the Oval Office. Cleland became the first Vietnam veteran to head the Veterans Administration. He was chairman of the President's Commission on the Disabled.

In 1982, he was elected Georgia secretary of state. He toured the state making speeches. He revved up a big voter-registration drive for Georgia's Super Tuesday primary last spring. It was a roaring success. At 46, Cleland was off and running for governor.

"It's my generation's turn," he said. "I'll be the first of the baby boomers to run. I'll be the first Vietnam vet. It's our turn to run things."

He planned to take on the Establishment. To battle the old hands of the Legislature, House Speaker Tom Murphy and the other graybeards who had run things since they seized power in 1966 and installed Lester Maddox as their puppet governor.

In the summer of 1988, the first polls showed Max Cleland was in a dead heat with Lt. Gov. Zell Miller for governor. The smiling, ever-ebullient Cleland was on his way. The election was still two years off.

In the background, trouble simmered. Shortly after his election to the state Senate in 1970, he was driving in his specially equipped car on Interstate 20 when he struck a pedestrian and killed her. The accident was ruled unavoidable and was hushed up. But it left Cleland feeling miserable and depressed.

His tenure as chief of the Veterans Administration received less than rave reviews. Veterans' organizations railed against him for showing little or no sensitivity to their causes. He was removed as head of the commission on the disabled before his term was up. Organizations representing disabled Americans denounced him for siding with the status quo in blocking efforts to make buildings accessible to the handicapped. The Carter administration saw him as a political liability. (Though by the time Jimmy Carter stood for re-election in 1980, the transgressions of Max Cleland seemed trivial compared with the other blunders of the Carter White House.)

Jane Fonda wrote Cleland a letter, asking his help in getting her a permit to act in a movie being made in New England. Veterans groups in Connecticut and Massachusetts opposed the idea of Fonda working there because she went to Hanoi during the Vietnam War and sided with the Communists. Cleland wrote the letter, saying let bygones be bygones, saying they ought to give Jane a work permit. Jane got her permit. The vets said they'd get even and quietly circulated petitions condemning Cleland as a cop-out.

Back in Georgia, lawyers grumped that Cleland's office was going to pot. He was not fulfilling his official duties, which included keeping up with corporate records and other data essential to making the state's legal machinery run smoothly.

"If the lawyers don't like him and think he's doing a rotten job, then he ought to put that fact in his elections brochure," one observer noted wryly. "That doesn't hurt Max. Nobody likes lawyers anyway."

Meantime, Cleland was getting a reputation among his employees as being arrogant and difficult to work for. He told his managers he didn't have time to run the office; he was out running for governor. Occasionally, he berated subordinates in front of outsiders, even journalists. He made enemies among those closest to him. His elections supervisor, Frances Duncan, applied for retirement. He fired his personal aide and driver, Paul Gregory.

He unknowingly made an enemy of longtime supporter, Lamar Weaver, a Cobb County insurance agent and a close pal of Gregory. Gregory knew too much about Cleland, and so did Weaver. In a statement to his attorney, Weaver said: "I met Cleland shortly after he was elected. We became friends. I was not only touting him for governor in 1990 but for president after that."

Cleland also was getting a reputation as a fellow who liked the ladies, liked them too much.

Weaver said in a statement to his attorney that he found a young woman "who had a crush" on Cleland and introduced them.

Shortly afterward, in the summer of 1988, Max Cleland, political powerhouse, became the butt of jokes and an object of ridicule in every corner of the state Capitol.

Tape recordings of conversations between Cleland and the woman who was Weaver's friend were played at political conventions and cocktail parties. Cleland's sexually explicit language, with the woman urging him on, brought snickers and wry grins.

Whether you had "heard the tapes" became a badge of status in political circles.

When the episode finally made the public prints, Cleland protested that the conversations were private dialogue between consenting adults and that his Democratic rivals were trying to smear him.

He was wrong on both counts. Public figures, especially those planning to run for governor against the powers-that-be, can't expect much privacy. Cleland's former friends and employees, not his Democratic colleagues, had fastened the secretary of state in their sights. Most of Cleland's political competitors wanted no part of the "smear."

"No. Don't tell me about it. I don't want to know. Please talk about something else," Lt. Gov. Zell Miller said frantically when a reporter tried to interview him.

"Tapes? What tapes?" asked House Speaker Tom Murphy when he was first approached about the matter.

Just as the buzz about the tapes subsided, Guy Davis, an Atlanta attorney who ran for governor in 1986 as a Republican, produced an affidavit from a woman who said she first met Cleland in 1981 when she was a "student reporter."

Davis refused to divulge her name and blotted it out on copies of her statement, in which she described in graphic detail aberrant sexual encounters with the triple amputee in his car at Stone Mountain and on a drive to Gordon County. She was the same unidentified woman who had taped Cleland's telephone calls. She said Lamar Weaver had advised her to record Cleland's phone calls.

Cleland protested again that his privacy had been breached. It had been; but by then, it didn't matter.

The question among statehouse pundits was no longer how Cleland would run as a gubernatorial candidate but who would run against him for secretary of state.

No one thought of Cleland, of course, as another Gary Hart, a daredevil philanderer. Instead, they thought of him as Max Cleland, bachelor triple amputee caught up in a miserable little sex episode that didn't even include intercourse.

"He must be a very lonely man," said a hard-eyed female state senator from north Fulton County.

So what does the downfall of Max Cleland in 1988 have to do with my departing a German railway station in 1956? Nothing much. Except it may illustrate as well as anything ever could the luck of the draw—a cruel difference that has left Max Cleland hurt and humiliated.

In 1997, Max Cleland was elected to the U.S. Senate to succeed Sam Nunn, who declined to seek re-election.

The Awakening

In 1990, George Berry, a career government bureaucrat, shocked most of his friends — and himself — by deciding to run for lieutenant governor. He was the guy everybody said ought to be mayor or governor or something. He turned out to be a less-than-spectacular candidate and ran third in the Democratic primary. State Sen. Pierre Howard won the lieutenant governor's post and the general election and immediately went to work on his campaign for governor in 1994 — a campaign which never occurred since Gov. Zell Miller decided to run for a second term. At this writing, Howard has given up his earlier plans to run for governor in 1998; Miller is planning to retire and write books, and Berry is a senior vice president at Cousins Properties in Atlanta, a position he won after losing his first political contest. He vows he will not seek public office again.

Atlanta Magazine — August 1990

George Berry couldn't believe it. Everybody seemed to smirk at him. Several citizens refused to be photographed with the once-respected and adored state commissioner of industry and trade. I must be dreaming, Berry thought. And this is a very bad dream.

People who once said they would do anything in the world to help him suddenly wouldn't return his phone calls. An old friend who gave a party in his honor handed him a bill for $2,000 for the food and beverages and suggested he pay it. Tears welled up in the eyes of his wife, Jeannine.

"What are we going to do?" she asked. For perhaps the first time in his adult life, George Berry was at a loss for an answer.

At age 53, his destiny appeared unclear. He was no longer gainfully employed. He wondered if he had made a wrong turn in a career course that just a few weeks before seemed certain. He had plunged into the pool of elective politics. He had several job offers in private enterprises, but he wanted to seek political office. At the last minute, he decided to enter the race for lieutenant governor of Georgia, a position so vacuous that candidates in past years have run on a platform of abolishing it.

As soon as he announced, he felt he had made a mistake.

"George is just having a late mid-life crisis," said one Berry watcher. "He's decided he may be too old to keep riding motorcycles. So he's going to run for office. He'll find out he can get his head busted doing that too."

Even Berry's closest buddies were stunned. How could Berry commit such a bizarre act? Run for political office? Was he out of his mind? He had betrayed his class, those cynical functionaries, journalists, and lawyers, who sat around second-guessing presidents and governors and mayors. Politicians were either crooks or chumps. Or both. They all knew that. Berry and his pals had agreed on that so often that it was no longer worth discussing.

Berry had sometimes given lip-service to those sentiments. He did not really believe them. He had to keep up appearances. After all, he had become a world-class bureaucrat. As city aviation commissioner, he had directed the construction and operation of new Hartsfield International Airport, the busiest airfield in the world. He had been Mayor Sam Massell's chief administrative officer. He had been a star appointment, as commissioner of Industry, Trade and Tourism, in the administration of Gov. Joe Frank Harris.

His bosses—Massell, Maynard Jackson, Harris—all liked Berry. He was a worker bee who knew his place. If things went well, they, the Elected Ones, got the credit. If things went awry, then the hired help, including Berry, took the heat.

Berry did as he was told, most of the time. He got fed up with corner cutting in the less-than-competent administration of Mayor Andrew Young. He left city government in 1983 to become a state official.

In business circles, many thought Berry was made of stuff better suited to making policy than simply implementing it.

Three years ago, State Democratic Party Chairman John Henry Anderson suggested Berry go for governor.

"We need a new face," he told him. "Look at that bunch of candidates. They're worn-out politicians. The public is tired of them."

Berry said no. In the summer of 1988, I wrote a piece for this magazine, saying Berry was a greater visionary than any gubernatorial candidate on the horizon.

The article angered Berry. "A good bureaucrat never tries to show up or look better than his boss. You may think that piece helped me. It didn't. It hurt," he said.

So Berry as a prospective candidate for governor was dropped from the list of topics for after-hours banter. Berry was locked in as an appointed public servant; he wanted to make certain everyone understood that.

Lt. Gov. Zell Miller promised to make Berry, his growing-up buddy from Young Harris College and the mountains, his executive secretary once Miller captured the governor's office.

Berry said he didn't know whether he was interested; but it was taken for granted he would snap up the job.

As the Harris administration began to wind down last spring, Harris' top appointees searched for new careers. Berry was the first to go.

A phone call from Sam Massell was an early clue that Berry was about to make a decision that would change his life.

"George says he's toying with the idea of running for lieutenant governor. Do you think he's serious?" asked the ex-mayor.

In the weeks that followed, Massell would repay Berry for his service to Massell and to the city. He would help raise, in lightning fashion, the big money Berry needed to wage a competitive campaign.

Berry phoned Joe Frank Harris and asked his advice about announcing for lieutenant governor.

"I can't take any part [in your campaign]. But if you don't run, you'll always wonder what might have happened if you had," Harris said.

Harris did not publicly help Berry's campaign. Yet several of Harris' firmest supporters went to the aid of the former commissioner.

Ed Harris (no kin to the governor), the retired Price Waterhouse executive who had formulated Harris' Quality Basic Education plan, became Berry's finance chairman. Most of the Harris-appointed members of the Board of Industry, Trade and Tourism pitched in to raise money and give advice. Computer mogul Jackie Ward, mentioned as a candidate for lieutenant governor last fall, became a co-chair of Berry's campaign.

Rival super-developers Tom Cousins (for whom Berry once worked) and John Portman went to the aid of the bureaucrat who dared run for elective office. Sam Williams, executive vice president of The Portman Companies, joined Berry's campaign steering committee. So did black entrepreneur Mack Wilbourn.

Berry phoned Zell Miller to seek his counsel. "I couldn't tell him what to do. On the one hand, you could argue it would hurt my campaign for governor, having someone that close to me running for governor. On the other hand, Berry was so well-liked that it might help me. But I told him, 'Don't worry about me. You have to do what you think is right for you.'"

In the days that followed Berry's announcement, Miller's well-heeled campaign organization would begin to help Berry. James Carville, Miller's professional campaign coordinator, recruited a top "hired gun" for Berry, one Gus Weill, 57, of Baton Rouge, La., who would handle Berry's media buys and work on campaign strategy.

If Berry (and Miller) could win the primary, the pair would mount an unprecedented state campaign as The Democratic Ticket against the Republicans in November.

Berry's connections to the business community might help populist Miller overcome the greatest threat to Democratic control of the Statehouse since 1966.

Miller was not alone among elected officials in promising help for Berry. Mayor Maynard Jackson said he would muster black votes for Berry. Agriculture Commissioner Tommy Irvin, though he faced minor GOP opposition himself, joined Berry's fund-raising efforts. Labor Commissioner Joe Tanner sent over his main political operative, Gary Horlacher, to manage Berry's campaign organization.

Still, not everything went Berry's way. His troubles and his doubts grew. He broke the Jimmy Carter rule. Berry didn't decide to run for office until the week before qualifying opened in April. Carter had established the precedent of stretching a campaign into a months- or even years-long affair. No serious candidate for high office had defied that rule since 1970 after Carter's successful four-year-long campaign for governor.

When Berry announced, seven other Democrats, several with extensive political backgrounds, already were in the race. An eighth Democrat, Rep. Frank Bailey of Clayton County, entered the contest behind Berry. Bailey thus deprived Berry of the important advantage in a field of obscure candidates of being listed first alphabetically on the ballot.

Sen. Pierre Howard, D-Decatur, would barely speak to Berry. Howard had counted on winning easily. A member of a rich and well-known family of lawyers, Howard relied on his old fraternity and tennis-team ties from the University of Georgia to pull him through. He also believed the black vote might go his way. Berry threatened to fragment that bloc.

"While he (Howard) was playing tennis at the University of Georgia, I was working my way through night school at Georgia State University," Berry remarked, and Howard sulked.

Berry's principal rival at the outset of the campaign was Senate President Pro Tem Joe Kennedy, D-Claxton, the epitome of the old-boy networkers who control Georgia government.

Kennedy had money, the support of the principal lobbying interests in the Capitol, and, most of all, the help of House Speaker Thomas Murphy, D-Bremen.

"When Joe is elected as lieutenant governor, me and him will run this state, no matter who is governor," Murphy confided.

Sen. Lawrence "Bud" Stumbaugh, D-Stone Mountain, pumped wads of his own cash into the campaign and spent barrels of money on getting out black voters, especially outside Atlanta.

Rep. Jim Pannell, D-Savannah, depended on a base of support in Savannah where he lived, in Atlanta where he grew up, and in northwest Georgia where several of his rich and influential relatives live.

On the Republican side, a 30-year-old lawyer, Matt Towery, was arrayed against former state Sen. Janice Horton and a schoolteacher, Ann Hall. Berry's close friend, former *Atlanta Constitution* Editor Hal Gulliver, a law partner of Towery, promised early to support the young Republican. He also tried to help Berry.

Berry found that many people he had counted on were already signed up with other candidates.

A few business leaders defected to Berry, but not as many as he had hoped.

In the opening days of the campaign, Berry felt depressed. He found the public attitude toward him had changed overnight. He was struck by the noticeable negative attitude of many people toward political candidates.

"Maybe it is a holdover from Watergate. I could see people smirk when they talked to me, as if I were doing something embarrassing," he said. "When I would pose for a photograph, some people would duck out of the picture. That never happened when I was Industry and Trade commissioner. They didn't want to be photographed with a political candidate."

Others wondered aloud why Berry had chosen to run for lieutenant governor.

"People would say, 'Why didn't you run for governor? Lieutenant governor is a nothing job. You're too good for that,'" Berry recalls.

He says he didn't seek election as governor because he did not wish to oppose his longtime ally, Miller. Others believe Berry, who came from an impoverished background in the mountains, felt insecure and unsure about going for the highest office in his first foray into politics.

If the obstacles in a campaign for lieutenant governor intimidated him, he would be overwhelmed by the complexities of a race for governor, he felt.

Why did he decide to do this awful thing of becoming a political candidate?

"I felt I had something to give. I felt I could make more of a difference in an elected office. I wanted to change my lifestyle. I wanted to see if I could do it," he says.

Would he enter the race again, now that he has felt rejection and the feeling of despair on the campaign trail?

"I am not sure. Yes, I guess I would. I had to know whether I could do it. Now I can tell my grandchildren I did it," he says.

Besides, he and Jeannine turned out to be a competent team of hand-shakers and back-slappers.

"You know, she keeps me going," says Berry. "She seems to actually enjoy this."

In early June, Berry took a long weekend off at the family retreat in rural Monroe County. "I lay awake listening to the birds and the night sounds, and I thought, 'This is wonderful.' This is what I would like to do, just stay down here where it is peaceful and quiet. I could rest and read.'"

The outcome of Berry's quest for elective office may tell us something about ourselves—whether we value competence in politics, how much the good-old-boy network counts for, and how much chance of survival an outsider has in the shark pool of insiders.

A few days after he was hired by Berry, Gus Weill, the media director of the campaign, sat in a courtyard of a restaurant and reminisced about his 33 years as a consultant.

"Occasionally, a truly exceptional candidate will come along, a man who is well-qualified for office and who has a résumé to back up what he can do," said Weill. "One such man is George Bush. George Berry might turn out to be like that. He is really well-qualified. He has the background to do a good job."

"Yes," noted an acquaintance, "but well-qualified candidates seldom win elections, especially here in the South."

"You're right," Weill said glumly. "The really well-qualified ones usually don't win."

As the primary campaign ended, Berry's stock as a potential winner picked up. The field of candidates was so big, however, that no one could even approach an accurate prediction about the outcome.

"I have found out something about politics I didn't know before," Berry said. "It is like a crapshoot; luck is more important than anything else."

Has Newt Grown Too 'National' For Georgia?

Syndicated column—September 16, 1990

Is Newt Gingrich gaining a higher national profile than Sam Nunn? Gingrich is quoted nearly every day by some national pundit on topics ranging from the state of the presidency to the plight of the homeless.

Television correspondents have interviewed the Georgia congressman in recent times in the Arabian Desert and on the banks of the Potomac, giving him an opportunity to say anything he wishes about nearly any subject that comes to mind.

Sixth District Rep. Newt Gingrich, the U.S. House Republican whip from Jonesboro, is articulate and ambitious. He clearly has his vision set far beyond the sales sheds of the Farmers Market and the clutter of Clayton County.

His election contest against Democrat challenger Dave Worley on Nov. 6 may test the notion that Georgians would rather have a Washington big-shot than a "homer" as their national representative.

Recent history suggests Georgia voters prefer high-profile national figures to carry their banner. Sen. Nunn, famous and influential on an international scale, is easily the most popular politician in the state. He is running for re-election with a war chest of nearly $1 million. Yet he has no opposition.

Armed Services Committee Chairman Nunn has been mentioned as a candidate for president in 1992 and seems to be gearing up to go for the nomination.

The late Sen. Richard Russell was a giant in Washington, as well as Armed Services Chairman.

There is more to the Nunn and Russell stories than national headlines. Both men brought to Georgia military installations and defense contracts that have spun off thousands of jobs and billions of dollars in purchasing power.

Gingrich can make no such claim. His district south of Atlanta ranks 405th out of 435 districts in the country in receiving federal funds, according to his opponent, Worley.

"That report (on federal spending in congressional districts) is five years old," says Gingrich's campaign chairman, Randy Evans. Even so, the 6th District ranks near the bottom of the federal pork barrel.

"Newt has gone Washington. He spends more time on CNN than he does in his district," says Kate Head, campaign manager for Worley.

Gary Koops of the national Republican Congressional Committee snaps back: "There aren't many congressmen who are on a first-name basis with the president."

You mean "The National Newt," as some unkind souls refer to Gingrich, addresses the president of the United States as "George?" Yup, says the GOP spokesman, although Gingrich is often President Bush's most vocal critic.

In recent days, Gingrich has been too busy to come home because he has been holed up at Andrews Air Force Base near Washington as part of the national budget summit. *The Wall Street Journal* has praised Gingrich as the brightest of the summiteers, advocating "growth-oriented tax measures." (By contrast, the *Journal* has described the other Georgia member of the summit, Sen. Wyche Fowler, as "a liberal" and "a tax wookie.")

Despite his busy-busy-busy schedule in Washington that has prevented him from returning to Jonesboro and environs, Gingrich has had time to go to West Virginia to debate a Democrat and has trips scheduled to Alabama and Wisconsin to help Republican candidates.

Still, Gingrich's local helpers and advisers, including West Georgia College Professor Mel Steely, get high marks for responding to constituents' problems in such nonglamorous categories as Social Security claims and veterans' benefits.

And Gingrich is favored to win re-election. But Worley will be no pushover. He has more PAC money than any other congressional challenger in the state. He won 44 percent of the vote against Gingrich in the 1988 presidential-year landslide for George Bush. Worley ran 10 points ahead of Democratic presidential nominee Michael Dukakis in the 6th District.

Suppose Gingrich wins again, then what? Insiders say he might be on his way to a Cabinet post or even be considered as a replacement for Dan Quayle for vice president.

"The whip is an extremely influential post," says GOP spokesman Koops. "Newt's predecessor, after all, is (Secretary of Defense) Dick Cheney."

Newt, of course, went on to lead the national Republican Revolution of 1994 and become speaker of the U.S. House of Representatives.

Bury My Bid at Burning Tree

Atlanta Magazine — May 1991

These are hard times for the Democratic Party, sharing the name of a national party that is following the Whigs and Federalists into the Valley of Irrelevance.

State Democrats are afflicted with the problem that plagued Georgia Republicans for years: no high-profile leadership.

Until Newt Gingrich came along, you were used to a Republican Party without a powerful chief. Being a party with no identifiable or influential leader was an essential part of the Georgia GOP profile. On the other hand, having the Georgia Democrats without a big gun on the national scene doesn't seem natural.

It's difficult to say exactly when the last Democratic kingpin fell, although we know his name: Sam Nunn. It may have been the day in January when Nunn, previously known as the nation's foremost military authority, balked at voting to go to war in the Persian Gulf.

Or it may have been the day in March when the easy war ended and the troops started flying home. Nunn was proved dead wrong.

Or was it two days later when Nunn announced he would not run for president, certainly not against George Bush?

Before his final exit from the presidential stage, Nunn had demurred repeatedly on invitations to the presidential games. But speaking to the Democratic Leadership Council meeting in Dallas as the war ended, Nunn said: "I am not running. I am not planning to run. I guess the only thing I could do short of a Sherman-like statement is rejoin Burning Tree," referring to his resignation in 1990 from the male-only golf club in Bethesda, Md.

In any event, Georgia has run out of heavy hitters on the national scene.

A case can be made that Nunn never has measured up to the likes of Walter George and Richard Russell in the Senate or Carl Vinson and Phil Landrum in the House or Jimmy Carter in the White House. (Come to think of it, there are those who say Jimmy Carter never measured up to Jimmy Carter in the White House.)

Washington pundits, most of whom are friendly to Nunn, say he is "very cautious." That is a polite way of saying "less than fearless."

Some thought he was on the verge of a nervous breakdown when he had to make a decision in 1987 on whether to support Robert Bork's nomination to the Supreme Court. In the end, he voted against Bork. He was nearly the last Democrat to cast his lot against the ultra-conservative jurist. He did so long after Bork's nomination was dead. Still, Nunn's vote against Bork stirred minor irritation at home.

At other points in his career, though, Nunn has appeared almost dashing in his courage.

When he first ran for the Senate in 1972, he assailed then-Gov. Jimmy Carter for turning his back on George Wallace and supporting George McGovern for president. This attack on Carter allowed Nunn, then a rich young lawyer from Perry, to break out of the pack of Democratic candidates and win the seat once held by Sen. Richard Russell.

Six years after his election, Nunn cast a vote in the Senate that was almost as startling as his anti-war vote last winter. In 1978, he voted with President Jimmy Carter to ratify the Panama Canal Treaties. He took the state's senior senator, Herman Talmadge, with him, kicking and screaming.

Nunn's vote "to give away the Panama Canal" stirred up almost as much criticism back in Georgia as did his anti-war vote. Letters of protest poured in from the home front. The Panama Canal issue contributed to the decline of Jimmy Carter, although historians may say those treaties saved the nation from prolonged strife in Central America.

Nunn's popularity returned in a few months, and he was back at the top of everybody's popularity poll in Georgia. Nunn was on friendly terms with the Defense Department, which poured billions of dollars into Georgia installations.

Nunn became the ranking Democrat on the Armed Services Committee, then chairman. It was just like the good old days—when his great-uncle, Carl Vinson, was chief of defense spending in the House, and Dick Russell parceled out military dollars from the Senate side. Under Nunn, Georgia was flush with defense funds and installations.

In 1989, Nunn was fierce in his opposition to former Sen. John Tower as secretary of defense in the Bush administration. Tower was to be among President Bush's first important Cabinet appointments. Tower had been a recent predecessor of Nunn's as chairman of the Armed Services Committee.

Nunn chopped down Tower for being too cozy with defense contractors, hard liquor and loose women. Nunn's success in upending Tower may have been the beginning of the decline of the National

Nunn. Republicans, many of whom had been friendly with him until then, turned suddenly cool toward the senior senator from Georgia.

On nearly every other matter, Nunn supported the Bush administration—until the Persian Gulf crisis erupted. His fidelity to Bush may have been more pragmatic than philosophical. After all, Bush swept Georgia and the rest of the South against the Democratic ticket in the presidential election of 1988. He figures to do the same in 1992.

When Nunn first raised doubts about our increasing presence in the Middle East, he found his supply of information from the Defense Department drying up.

That lack of sound intelligence may account for his misjudgment on the war.

In retrospect, the White House must have known from the start that Saddam Hussein, with his World War I tactics and his second-rate Soviet hardware, was never a match for a high-tech military machine designed to fight a superpower in a "future world" war.

Nunn apparently was unaware we were facing a pushover. His miscalculation on the Persian Gulf War also undermined his opposition to President Reagan's "Star Wars" Strategic Defense Initiative. The successful Patriot anti-missile missile, used in the Gulf, refuted the notion that "you can't shoot a bullet with a bullet."

Of course, Nunn could never have seriously entertained a campaign for the presidency. Even if Bush's popularity turned sour, Nunn still could not win the White House, because he could not win his party's nomination. He lacks liberal credentials; he is a Johnny-come-lately on domestic issues; he doesn't hobnob with the Eastern Liberal Establishment.

His failure to make the cut in the presidential pre-warmups is not the root cause of his diminished stature. After all, Richard Russell in the 1950s and '60s was in much the same position. Russell might have had a shot at the White House—in another time and another place, flying a banner other than Democrat or Dixiecrat. Even without the presidency as a possibility, Russell remained a mighty national force.

What happened to Nunn? Perhaps he simply lost touch with home. He forgot his constituency. He went national, then international. At the 1988 Democratic National Convention in Atlanta, Nunn considered hosting a party for the Washington press corps with no locals invited. He obviously believed his base of power was on the world stage, not in the backwaters of Georgia.

Nunn is not the first eminent Georgian to forget his roots. In the 1950s, Sen. Walter George, as chairman of the Foreign Relations Committee, became the Senate's foremost authority on international issues. He had little time for Georgia. When he came home to prepare for a contested re-election campaign, he found that many of his longtime supporters had retired or died. He thought his old-time supporters were still ready to rally to his cause until he tried to call them and they didn't answer. He quit the Senate.

Herman Talmadge quickly picked up his mantle. There are no such apparent Democratic successors to Nunn waiting in the wings to take center stage as the senior senator fades back among the spear-carriers.

The junior senator, Wyche Fowler, is too liberal to take Nunn's place as Georgia's most beloved and influential politician.

Governor Zell Miller has the right stuff. He has promised to quit the governor's office after one term, but he'll be in his 60s then. That is probably too late to start a march to the pinnacles of national power.

Ninth District Rep. Ed Jenkins, D-Jasper, is in tune with his region. Yet he is far from being close to the liberal Democratic leadership of the House. As a result, he has been hobbled in attempts to exert national influence.

The truth is, with Nunn shunted aside, Georgia has no nationally ranked political players, except a Republican. Newt Gingrich of Jonesboro may be the Russell-George-Vinson-Nunn of the future.

Sure, he barely won re-election in 1990. Remember though, his close call was a fluke, the result of not paying close enough attention to what was going on in his district. The narrow victory got his attention. He now spends much time working on down-home matters. Gingrich may have difficulty in the reapportionment session of the Georgia Legislature later this summer. Some Democrats undoubtedly will try to draw a congressional district for Gingrich in which he cannot win re-election. A coalition of Republican and black legislators, rattling legal papers and going to court, won't let that happen.

House Minority Leader Bob Michel of Illinois is expected to retire next year, and Gingrich is likely to succeed him. Gingrich's end ambition, he says, is to become speaker of the U.S. House.

A Republican-majority House with Gingrich as speaker—now that would be a real power position.

The next Great Georgian could be a member of the GOP, a onetime gadfly college professor from Carrollton.

He would fit right in. Demographics are on his side. The suburbanites and baby boomers are moving to the front.

Just think of it, there would be The Newt as our point man on the national scene. He would be there to take issue with the president on how to reinvigorate the economy. He would never see a war he didn't like or a treaty he did. He would denounce constantly the declining

Democrats as "traitors and weaklings." Every time we flicked on C-SPAN, there would be Newt.

On second thought, Nunn may not be so bad. He won re-election without opposition in 1990. Of course, that was before he turned out to be a dove in hawk's feathers. Still, he could be rehabilitated. Even if Sam Nunn has lost his clout, he is still a nice man. He is certainly no Newt Gingrich.

Fall from Grace

Atlanta Magazine—June 1991

Until the spring of 1991, Professor Abe Ordover was the Joe Montana of the Emory University Law School. He was its superstar. He was an inspiration to aspiring trial lawyers. He had established Emory as the pre-eminent center for learning to litigate. His trial-preparation program drew attorneys, judges and legal scholars from across the country. He held the prestigious L. Q. C. Lamar chair at the law school. Ordover was a handsome, keen-witted lawyer-turned-teacher, generally admired by Atlanta's legal community.

Emory's higher-ups believed they were fortunate to have such a man on their faculty. He gave their institution a national name.

But the professor had a problem. By the time the first dogwoods budded in March, many in Emory's administration wished they had never heard of the 54-year-old Ordover. His perceived problem had consumed him. His career was in tatters. He was jobless and seeing a psychiatrist and appealing for anonymity.

Students charged Ordover with sexual harassment. They said he gave women "special attention." Ordover's accusers were officially nameless. A committee of his peers investigated the accusations and cleared him of wrongdoing. Students protested and boycotted. The case was reopened. Ordover was reprimanded, then resigned under pressure.

Emory agreed to pay him more than $1 million to keep his mouth shut and promise not to sue, according to a reliable source at the school.

In an hour-long interview, several days after his resignation, Ordover refused to talk about the settlement. But he says he was betrayed by Emory and stunned by its handling of the unsigned charges against him. In that regard, he may have a point.

"I felt like the Russian political prisoner who is sentenced to an insane asylum," he says. "The situation was beyond recognizable reality. I had to resign to save my sanity."

What is the truth about Ordover? Is he a man brought down by malicious false accusations leveled in secrecy by failing students in his classroom? Or is he just another dirty old man who likes to put his hands on nubile young things flitting about the college campus? Did his long-rumored amorous ways with students finally catch up with him? Or was he wrongly accused and destroyed in a way we have not witnessed since Sen. Joseph McCarthy and his red witch-hunters passed from the scene?

By his own admission, Ordover is "a touchy-feely" person. That means he is liable to put his hands on you during conversation, put his arm around your shoulder, tap you on the chest, or slap you on the back while he is talking. He is that way with men as well as women.

There's not much doubt Ordover likes females. He says he "gave a lot of attention to women" in his classes. His detractors say "a lot of attention" rates as the understatement of the year.

"I take women [students] seriously. I am sympathetic to their aspirations," he says. That is as far as it went, he maintains. He did not use his position of power to gain sexual favors. He says that over and over.

Still, rumors about Ordover's sexual misbehavior have cropped up several times during his 10-year tenure at Emory. Word got around that he was caught having sex in a car with a female student at a deserted shopping center on Cobb Parkway. He was seen in a passionate embrace with a student in the parking lot of a fashionable Atlanta restaurant. No first-hand sightings, mind you, but that was the talk. Ordover himself had heard it. He says that a year ago he asked Assistant Law School Dean Susan Sockwell to let him know if she heard any "reports" of his association with female students. He said he wanted to take steps to stop the talk. She said she'd let him know.

If Ordover indeed kept his distance from his women students, then why the rumors?

In a letter in defense of Ordover to Emory President James T. Laney, a former student, Atlanta attorney Robert C. Koski, wrote:

"Something I did note during my time at Emory was that Mr. Ordover's personal style did not have a uniformly positive effect. Some students considered him to be too cocky, too sure of himself, too aggressive in class, too confident in his knowledge, too critical of their responses, too well-dressed, too physically fit, and otherwise threatening. Some students had such a distaste for his style as to be suspicious of him.

"Whether this was from envy, some perceived personal slight, or for just cause, I could rarely say for certain. This kind of animosity also showed itself in a destructive way in what I call 'the rumor mill.' On a number of occasions, I heard statements suggesting that Professor Ordover had romantic attachments or involvements with certain students. When I confronted persons making these suggestions, I discovered that every person making such an allegation had absolutely no personal knowledge of such activities, but merely suspected it about his relationship with one coed or another. I later discovered from conversations with some of the women alleged to be involved, who were often my friends, that there was nothing to the allegations, and that the relationships were socially and academically proper."

Ordover says students sometimes misunderstood his motives when he attempted to be friendly. He once offered a female student tickets to an Atlanta Hawks basketball game that he and his wife had decided to pass up. He says the student believed mistakenly that Ordover wanted to escort her to the ball game.

Interestingly, Ordover says he was told that all the complaints against him came from students in his freshman civil procedures course; there were no complaints from students in his second-year evidence class or from graduate courses.

"First-year law students are nervous and suspicious of everything and everybody," says an old hand at teaching law at Emory and the University of Georgia. "They came from schools where they were outstanding students. Now they are in classes where every student is 'outstanding.' That takes some getting used to."

Still, doubt lingers. Michael Dowd, a New York attorney and director of legal advocacy and training for the New York State Office for the Prevention of Domestic Violence, phoned a woman public-relations executive in Atlanta to try to get media support for his friend Ordover. The PR executive says she made "a few phone calls" about Ordover's background and decided not to accept the assignment. She would not elaborate on what she discovered. She also said she did not want her name associated in any way with the Ordover controversy.

This points up a key issue in the case: Ordover's critics and accusers want anonymity; it is only his supporters who are willing, even eager, to attach their names to their comments.

Professor Ordover is not a low achiever. His résumé dazzles. It contains a yard-long list of awards, publications and film productions regarding his trial-law work. A 1961 graduate of the Yale University Law School, Ordover practiced 10 years in Manhattan with the firm of Cahill, Gordon & Reindel. He was part of the team that represented Trans-World Airlines in its years-long legal battle against eccentric billionaire Howard Hughes. As counsel for Empire Trust Co., Ordover took on in court the notorious Roy Cohn and won a $150,000 judgment in a case involving a defaulted loan. He represented NBC in a celebrated lawsuit challenging the FCC's fairness doctrine. He lost that one.

He was teaching law at Hofstra University on Long Island when Emory recruited him in 1981. Emory put him in charge of the administration of the NITA (National Institute for Trial Advocacy) trial-techniques program. His duties included recruiting 225 lawyers, judges, and law professors to work in the NITA program.

He produced 50 films at Emory on trial procedures. He made Emory shine in legal circles everywhere.

His plight has elicited a stack of testimonials, as thick as the city directory, from colleagues around the country.

"Abe is the greatest guy in the world. He inspires you to try your best. He is a natural leader and smart as hell," says Lake Rumsey, an Atlanta trial lawyer who teaches at Emory and has written a textbook on trial techniques.

"He is now the heart and soul of the litigation program, and the litigation program is the heart and soul of the national recognition of our law school," Dr. Phillip G. Benton wrote to Emory President Laney. Benton is an Emory-educated physician who also is a graduate of the law school and a member of its adjunct faculty for nearly 10 years.

Yet, throughout Ordover's time at Emory, whispers were mixed with the applause. In January, the whispering grew louder. The first sexual-harassment complaints were lodged against Ordover in the office of Assistant Law School Dean Sockwell. Ordover says he was not informed.

The Ordover file was turned over to Robert Etheridge, assistant vice president for equal opportunity programs at Emory.

Law School Dean Howard O. "Woody" Hunter also was notified. He appointed two law school professors and a medical school faculty member to investigate Ordover's conduct. Ordover says he had no idea he was being investigated.

(Ironically, as soon as word of the investigation circulated, rumors sprang up about the investigators. One of Ordover's "judges" had been married to two of his students. Or so the rumor went.)

Between March 1 and April Fool's Day, Abe Ordover's glory disintegrated into scandal and protest. This chronology is based on Ordover's recollection and supplemented by published reports and correspondence. Dean Hunter declined to comment.

MARCH 1: Dean Hunter summons Ordover to his office, presents him with a list of accusations (but not the names of his accusers), and suspends him from teaching.

As he walked from Hunter's office, Ordover says he "felt numb." He had a sense he was finished at Emory.

Ordover hires noted New York trial lawyer Jo Ann Harris to represent him.

MARCH 7-8: The Ordover committee takes 25 hours of testimony against the professor. Ordover is not allowed in the hearing room. After a fuss, his lawyer is admitted. She is not permitted to cross-examine witnesses and is admonished not to reveal the identity of Ordover's accusers, not even to her client.

On Friday, March 8, Ordover spends four hours, from 8:00 P.M. until midnight, before the committee, telling his side of the story. No, he hadn't sexually harassed anyone. No, he hadn't tampered with exam scores to help favored students. No, he didn't know what this was all about.

MARCH 15: Dean Hunter informs Ordover at 11:30 A.M. that he has been cleared of all charges. His investigators report they found not a shred of evidence to support the most serious charge, that he rigged exam scores to help attractive female students. Hunter lifts Ordover's suspension and tells him to resume teaching his classes—except the first-year civil procedures course.

There are no reprimands and no sanctions imposed on Ordover. Before they depart, on what Ordover recalls as friendly terms, Hunter offers him a little advice: "Keep your door open during conferences with female students. … Be careful."

Emory issues a press release clearing Ordover's name.

MARCH 18: When Ordover goes to his office, he finds a memo from Hunter, informing the faculty of the all-clear findings of the Ordover investigation.

Dean Hunter schedules a meeting with Ordover's civil procedures class at 11:00 A.M. to discuss the outcome of the investigation. Hunter is met by a storm of vehement protests, challenging the investigators' findings.

By the time 3:00 P.M. rolls around, the campus is in an uproar. At a "town meeting" of students, Hunter faces an unruly crowd of epithet-hurling students.

He tries to calm them. He announces Emory has not yet decided to accept the findings of the investigative committee. He promises the inquiry will continue. He repeats his retreat later that afternoon in a TV interview.

At 6:00 P.M., a weary and visibly shaken Hunter shows up in Ordover's office. He informs the professor that indeed he will be reprimanded for his conduct.

MARCH 19: Students march on President Laney's office. A boycott of classes begins. However, Ordover reports that 90 percent of his students were present in his second-year evidence class.

Late that afternoon, Ordover receives a copy of the reprimand and official orders on how to conduct himself in the presence of students. The document reads in part:

"Do not have individual conferences in your office with female students with the door closed … [or] after normal business hours. … Do not invite individual female students to lunch or dinner, to go jogging, to go to an arts event or to go to a sports event. … When conferring with a female student about an examination, a paper, a class assignment or some other matter in your office, do not sit on the same side of the desk.

"It should go without saying that you should not kiss, hug, stroke hair or otherwise touch a female student except in a manner in which you would touch another professional person of either sex, such as by shaking hands."

In his letter to Ordover, Dean Hunter adds: "Finally, I request that you seek appropriate counseling to develop a better understanding of the ways in which your behavior is perceived by others. I expect to be informed of the nature and extent of this counseling, although the substance should, of course, remain confidential between you and your counselor."

Meanwhile, student protest leaders meet with representatives of the Emory administration. A new investigative committee is to be appointed. A new investigation will be launched. New charges of misconduct are brought against Ordover.

MARCH 20: A committee of Atlanta attorneys, many of them leaders of the state Bar, visit Hunter on Ordover's behalf. Nothing comes of the meeting.

MARCH 21: Ordover announces he is taking a temporary leave of absence until June 1. "I cannot teach in chaos; nor can I expect serious students to learn," he says.

"A few students who apparently have no respect for their fellow students, their dean, their faculty and the reputation of this law school have been permitted to create chaos. This atmosphere promotes unrest, generates more false charges and makes rational resolution of disputes impossible," he said in a prepared statement.

MARCH 25: Emory lawyers turn down a proposal by Ordover's counsel to try to mediate the dispute and cool off the campus. "The situation is irretrievable," an Emory spokesman tells Jo Ann Harris.

Negotiations begin on how to let Ordover exit the scene—and provide him financial compensation in exchange for not filing lawsuits against Emory and his still-anonymous student accusers.

MARCH 31: On Easter Sunday, Ordover returns to a quiet campus to clean out his desk and leave Emory behind.

APRIL 1: Abraham Philip Ordover resigns, effective June 1, as L. Q. C. Lamar professor of law and director of litigation programs at the Emory University School of Law.

APRIL 2: The board of directors of the Atlanta Bar asks Ordover to direct its modest summer education program. He says he would be happy to oblige.

"In the face of all this adverse publicity, it took guts for them to ask me to do that," Ordover says.

The one-time luminary of the Emory law school faculty now spends his time puttering around the house. Carol, his wife of 30 years, teaches fifth grade at Lovett School. Ordover speaks proudly of his two grown sons, one a budding playwright, the other a bright beginning journalist. The professor, who is an accomplished amateur photographer, is organizing a late-spring show of his pictures. He also is trying to shake off a deep depression. He has sought psychiatric counseling. He fears his reputation has been spoiled forever.

The specific sins of Abe Ordover are not clear. No criminal charges were ever lodged against him, not even in the angry, hysterical atmosphere that surrounded his final days at Emory. Yet the perception exists that Ordover was too cozy with some women in his classes. The truth of that may never be known.

Dean Hunter was quoted recently in the *National Law Journal* as describing the Ordover episode as "a quite useful learning experience. We might end up with some better lawyers as a result."

Paul C. Kurland, a prominent New York attorney and friend of Ordover, took exception to Hunter's remarks. In a letter to Emory, he wrote:

"What have Emory law students learned? Perhaps they learned that if you are not satisfied with the outcome of a hearing, trial, tribunal or other litigated matter, the proper response is to boycott, threaten and intimidate those involved in the decision-making process. Is that how they will react the first time they receive an adverse decision from a court? They may have also learned that when those in authority are weak, indecisive and back away from announced decisions, people are not brought together to make positive, meaningful changes, reconcile and work things out. In such circumstances, a few loud voices intent upon destroying a wonderful teacher and damaging for many years the reputation of an esteemed institution are permitted to rule and dominate."

So Abe Ordover joins the growing number of male authority figures brought down by charges of sexual harassment. Was he guilty of indiscretion in dealing with female students? Perhaps.

Was he treated even-handedly by Emory? No. Emory chose to sacrifice Ordover's career to the hysteria of a mob motivated by rumors and charges not proved. The school paid Ordover handsomely for promising not to bring lawsuits against the institution or the accusing students.

Why did Emory officials not take immediate steps in January to remove Ordover from the center of a smoldering conflict before it became a public controversy? Why was mediation and counseling not arranged for both sides in the earliest stages of the problems?

Emory offers no answers, and Ordover only guesses at their motives.

It may have involved no more than a string of wrong decisions and finally a wish to end the negative publicity. "I am not granting any more interviews [on the Ordover episode]," Dean Hunter said when asked for an explanation.

Another instructive note: Lawyers and former students, men and women, were eager to be identified in the defense of Ordover. Dozens wrote letters of recommendation for Ordover. Leading lawyers phoned to describe the talents of the ousted professor. Others publicly resigned from the Emory litigation program in protest of his punishment.

Yet not a single one of his critics or accusers—the people who destroyed his career—was willing to have his or her name attached to the case.

Ordover founded a mediation/arbitration firm in Atlanta and, at this writing, continues to be one of the bright minds in the legal profession.

His Honor

Atlanta Magazine — August 1991

Georgia Supreme Court Justice Charles Weltner deserved the Kennedy Library Foundation's Profiles in Courage award that he received in Boston a couple of months ago. But he won it for the wrong reason.

The Kennedy family said it wanted to cite Weltner for his courage in quitting Congress rather than appear on the Democratic ballot with racist Lester Maddox in the 1966 election. Few Georgia observers believe that was Charles Longstreet Weltner's finest hour. He has built a reputation for bravery and achievement on more solid stuff than retreating from Maddox.

• Weltner was the first member of the House Committee on Un-American Activities to insist on a full-scale investigation of the Ku Klux Klan in the 1960s.

The Weltner inquiry sent Robert Shelton, the imperial wizard of the Klan, to prison for contempt of Congress and began the demise of the KKK as a force in the South.

• As a state Supreme Court justice, Weltner has authored significant decisions affecting public accountability and conflicts of interest.

"A bribe is a bribe is a bribe" even if it is a duly reported political campaign contribution, Justice Weltner said in describing one anti-corruption opinion. Legislators and lobbyists were dismayed.

• As a Superior Court judge, he was stern and fair. He turned tough in handing out long sentences to habitual criminals. He made his liberal friends wince when he openly advocated use of the death penalty in some cases.

• He began the renewal of his education in 1980. He has mastered a half-dozen archaic Semitic languages. He speaks fluent Spanish and can read and translate German. He is a candidate for a doctoral degree at Trinity College in Dublin, Ireland. He has written a couple of books and may write another one. He is a student of the roots of Western civilization in the Middle East.

So what is Charlie Weltner's proudest achievement in his productive life?

"I am sort of proud of recovering so far from cancer. I am proud of the progress I am making and the insights that have come from having a really bad case of anything," he says.

A year ago (August 1990), Weltner discovered he had cancer of the esophagus. He was told his chances of recovery were poor.

He remembers:

"I was having difficulty swallowing. I had heard that was something that needed to be checked out. Because it might be related to cancer.

"I went to the doctor, and he did all these tests and found I had a tumor on my esophagus. He told me it could be scar tissue. But I suspected it might be cancer.

"And then the man who took the biopsy said it looked 'viable' to him. I said, 'What does that mean?' He said, 'Viable means having a tendency to be cancer.'

"He [the doctor] called me the next afternoon, about three o'clock, and said, 'We got the tests back, and it's cancer.' And I said, 'Well, what do I do now?'"

Weltner underwent surgery, then radiation treatment and chemotherapy. His hair fell out, and his weight fell from 155 pounds to 128. He thought he would soon die.

His tale continues:

"At first, I thought it was inevitable. For the first three days, I sort of stayed in the grave. I thought it was over.

"I was fortunate to have a friend who convinced me that the odds quoted to me don't mean anything because they don't distinguish between who lives and dies.

"That friend was Wyche Fowler."

Sen. Wyche Fowler Jr. is Weltner's political protégé. He served as Weltner's chief assistant in the Congress. Weltner has been Fowler's No. 1 adviser in Fowler's climb from the Atlanta Board of Aldermen to assistant floor leader of the United States Senate. Now the student has become the teacher.

Weltner: "Wyche said the people who live with cancer are the people who decide to live. [He said] the people who decide to live are the people who have something to live for. 'You've got something to live for. You owe it to people to live on.'

"That conversation created a total reversal in my mental attitude. Since that time, I have just believed I was going to survive.

"My father lived 94 years. And I was just 62. So I said, 'Well, I've got 32 more years.' I had always planned to live a long time."

Weltner's father, Philip, was the second chancellor of the University System of Georgia and a president of Oglethorpe University. He counseled Weltner to quit the House of Representatives in 1966 rather than support the Georgia Democratic ticket that included segregationist gubernatorial candidate Lester Maddox. Philip Weltner died in 1981.

Not all Charles Weltner's friends have been as confident of his survival and longevity as Wyche Fowler.

Awards and recognition were suddenly heaped upon him. The Profiles in Courage prize was just one accolade that came his way. In November, he was presented the prize for legal scholarship by the Harvard Law School Association of Georgia. The award had not been given to anyone in six years. In May, Weltner received the Logan E. Bleckley Award of the Litigation Section of the Atlanta Bar Association. In June, Resurgens Atlanta presented him its 1991 Race Relations Award. His portrait was unveiled in the Fulton County courthouse in July.

"These awards are given to me in the mistaken belief I am going to die," Weltner chuckles. "Back in November (when he received the Harvard award), I was in bad shape. I imagine the selection process for that award went something like this: 'If we're going to do something for this guy, we'd better do it in a hurry.'"

Shortly after Weltner's cancer was discovered, his friend and former law partner, Atlanta attorney Charles Kidd, decided to have a physical checkup to make sure he was OK. He was not. Cancer was diagnosed in two places in Kidd's body. One form of the malady would have killed him shortly.

"We talked many times about it," says Weltner. "We are good friends and we support each other."

Kidd's cancer is in remission. He is back practicing law and playing tennis.

To others suffering with possibly fatal cancer, Weltner would pass on Fowler's advice:

"Do not let those expletive-deleted experts tell you anything about odds. Because they don't know anything about odds. All they know is that, over some period of time, some people who have it have died — and some of them have lived. For everybody who has lived, the odds are 100 percent in their favor.

"It is a question of whether or not you want to live. That is determined by whether you've got anything worth living for.

"If you want to die peacefully and say, 'Well, I am going to heaven now,' you can do that. But if you decide, by God, you want to stick around a while, you can do that, too."

Weltner says he is interested in writing another book, this one about the development of civilization on the Arabian peninsula, but he has little enthusiasm for producing a volume on his fight against cancer.

"People gave me these books on how to survive and all that. I didn't read a word of them. It is so much a matter of personal resolve, which is a mixture of a whole lot of things. I don't know that my experience is of interest to anybody or of value to anybody.

"It would require a lot of real exposure of my internal feelings. I am not particularly anxious to do that."

Before Weltner's illness was diagnosed, word was out that he was bored on the Supreme Court bench and intended to resign.

"It has been true with me, unfortunately, that my attention span is not what it should be," he says. "I made no secret of the fact that after four years or so on the Superior Court, I was frustrated with the repetitiveness and an accumulation of things. Today was just like yesterday. This week was just like last week.

"I have not felt that way on the Supreme Court because we keep doing things that are different. You don't have to try the same case over and over and over. ... But I am approaching 10 years service. And that is a long time. I feel a sense of frustration in this job. I have been here much longer than I have been in any other job," he says.

After dropping out of the 1966 congressional race, Weltner tried for a comeback in 1968 and was defeated. He ran for mayor of Atlanta in 1973 and came in third.

Gov. George Busbee appointed him to the Superior Court in 1976, then elevated him to the Supreme Court in 1981.

Weltner has been wed three times, divorced twice and has sired six children, ranging from 9 to 39 years old.

He says he refuses to revisit his decision in 1966 to leave the House or consider whether he might now be sitting in Wyche Fowler's place in the Senate.

"The worst thing that could happen is to have regrets and doubts. The 5th Congressional District (Atlanta) has been, ever since 1962, a hazardous place. I doubt I would have survived the winds and waves of partisan politics. I do not think I could have been elected to the Senate, simply because I am not as good a campaigner as Wyche, and he won by a hair—22,000 votes. Wyche has political talents that I never had."

Weltner is not home free in his battle with The Big C. His treatment was discontinued in January. His doctors said he appeared to be free of cancer in the spring. His hair has grown back.

In June, he still weighed only 134 pounds and said his energy had not fully returned.

He is second in line to become chief justice of Georgia—a position his maternal great-great-grandfather, Joseph Henry Lumpkin, held in the 1860s.

Weltner is not counting yet on moving up to that highest post in the Georgia judiciary, though he says "it is something my grandchildren might enjoy."

"I am planning on being here for my six-month checkup. I have made no plans ahead of that," he says.

Charles Weltner died August 31, 1992, shortly after being named chief justice of Georgia.

Bowers' Career Could Turn on Lesbian Controversy

Syndicated column — October 9, 1991

Attorney General Mike Bowers calls Georgia's criminal justice system rotten and says the Pardons and Paroles Board is turning out droves of dangerous criminals. No one pays much attention.

He says democracy may collapse if the state loses a lawsuit attacking majority elections. Yawns break out.

He claims a plane used by a former National Guard commander was involved in dope smuggling. Who cares?

He prosecutes a multimillion-dollar price-fixing case involving the sale of milk to schools. So what?

Finally, the attorney general commits an act that gets rapt public attention, though not many raves from his Democratic colleagues. Bowers decides he doesn't want to hire a female Emory law school graduate because she is marrying another woman.

A firestorm of criticism erupts. How could Bowers dare not hire a lesbian lawyer? his critics demand.

He is called a tyrant, a trampler on First Amendment rights, an invader of privacy.

Gays, lesbians, and the American Civil Liberties Union are planning to sue Bowers. The Emory University Law School says he can't recruit there anymore.

Bowers' political career may rise or fall on his decision not to give Robin Shahar a $36,000-a-year job representing the taxpayers of the state. Bowers is plainly on a course that might take him into the governor's race in 1994.

He also is on a collision course with Lt. Gov. Pierre Howard, the favorite of many Capitol insiders to succeed Zell Miller as governor.

Howard is noncontroversial, unabrasive, and a bona fide bourbon Democrat. He has used his office to make friends and prepare for the gubernatorial race of 1994. He carved out legislative and congressional districts in the special session of the Legislature that were designed to assist his buddies, even Republican ones.

State Sen. Don Johnson, D-Royston, state Sen. Arthur "Skin" Edge, R-Newnan, and former state Rep. Johnny Isakson, R-Marietta, are beholden to Howard for aiding them at reapportionment time.

At the moment, Gov. Miller seems to be leaning toward helping Howard become governor. Miller is at odds with Bowers.

Miller has tapped Howard to stand in for him at several important ceremonies. While Miller was traveling abroad, he invited Howard and his family to spend a weekend in the Governor's Mansion. (Gov. Joe Frank Harris never offered such courtesies to Lt. Gov. Zell Miller. But then Harris did not support Miller for governor.)

Miller has let it be known that relations between him and Bowers are strained. He has criticized Bowers' handling of the execution of convicted murderer Warren McCleskey. He says he doesn't need Bowers' advice in settling a lawsuit on how Georgia elects its judges. He says Bowers passes the buck too often.

Barely two years ago, Bowers informed Republican candidate recruiters that he had no interest in switching parties or in running for governor. "I will not run for governor as long as Zell Miller is a candidate," he said. "I will not run against my friend." Besides, he said, he was a lifelong Democrat.

Now Bowers finds himself without the friendship of Miller and with diminishing support among mainstream Democrats. His stubborn defense of majority election of judges has alienated many black leaders, all of whom are Democrats. His tough law-and-order rhetoric and his advocacy of the death penalty have turned off liberal Democrats. He has always been at odds with the Democratic leadership of the state House.

The lesbian controversy may be the last straw. Activist homosexual organizations and feminist groups, whose members nearly all are card-carrying Democrats, have Bowers in their sights.

He may find there is no room left for him in the Democratic Party. And 1994 could see Bowers turning Republican and taking on the Democratic establishment and Lt. Gov. Howard.

Bowers switched to the Republican Party in 1993. He resigned as attorney general on June 1, 1997, to run for governor. On June 5, 1997, he announced he had participated in an extramarital affair of more than a decade with a one-time employee. In one of the most astonishing political developments in memory, he also labeled himself a hypocrite. The gay and lesbian community celebrated.

An Eye for Dollars

Georgia Trend – February 1992

If you're sick of wearing eyeglasses and don't mind traveling, has Wayne Smith got a deal for you.

All you have to do is agree to go to Russia, get an eye exam here, and hand the Rev. Mr. Smith a check for five grand.

Then, voila! You're off to Moscow for a week. You'll be met at the airport by an English-speaking guide. A Chaika limousine will whisk you to a four-star Austrian-managed hotel where the leaders of the late Communist Party once convened. You can attend the Bolshoi Ballet, gamble at the Casino Royale, dine on fine food, and tour the Kremlin.

You'll be introduced to Dr. Svyatoslav N. Fyodorov, the world-famous ophthalmologist, who will supervise surgery on your eyes that he guarantees will leave you with near-perfect vision. Before you exit mother Russia, you can toss away your spectacles and see the sights. At least that is what Parson Smith and Dr. Fyodorov claim.

All for just $5,000. You can take along your spouse for another $2,500. No rubles, please. Just dollars.

For no extra charge, you can see the bread lines, barter with black marketeers on the Arbot, and witness the chaos of Russia in the throes of a food shortage, a collapsed government, and a new revolution – all without the inconvenience of getting involved.

This see-Moscow-and-see deal may sound like an off-the-wall Comedy Club routine. Or a fast-talking come-on by con artists traveling in the guise of cleric/medical authorities.

But D. Wayne Smith is no Jim Bakker and S. N. Fyodorov no quack. Smith, a Presbyterian preacher, is as legitimate as they come. He is founder and president of the Atlanta-based Friendship Force, a 15-year-old cultural exchange program started under the aegis of President Jimmy Carter. Smith counts among his friends some of Georgia's leading businesspeople and politicians. His vision correction project in Russia has the blessing of Gov. Zell Miller, not noted for being suckered. Miller had his eyes fixed in the mid-1980s at Emory by a surgeon who had studied under Fyodorov. And Fyodorov himself operated on Smith's eyes in Moscow.

As for the 64-year-old Fyodorov, he is the "world's leading eye surgeon and the father of the space-age miracle of 'infrakeratoplasty.'"

That's roughly his description of himself. In the future, he hopes to become known for a cell rejuvenation therapy that he says will extend people's lives. He also doesn't mind telling you that he made $5 million "hard currency" in profit last year.

His long list of attributes does not include modesty. Surprisingly, many of Fyodorov's professional colleagues in the United States agree with his high opinion of himself, though some are skeptical of his boasts of a near-perfect record of turning old eyes into new ones.

"Early in the next century, eyeglasses will become obsolete," says a leading Atlanta eye surgeon. "Fyodorov will be remembered as the man who made that possible." His procedure involves changing the shape of the cornea with the help of a computer, dye, an electron microscope and surgeon's scalpel.

Fyodorov is scheduled to come to Georgia this winter as the guest of developer Tom Cousins. He will hunt quail with Gov. Miller and other high rollers on Cousins' plantation near Albany. Among the invited guests: Sam Walton, billionaire owner of the Wal-Mart stores.

The Russian doctor is said to be considering opening up a branch of his eye clinic in Georgia. That causes American medical officials to frown. That's OK. Fyodorov frowns right back. He calls the American Medical Association "a medical mafia" that has held back healing in the U.S.

Fyodorov is more than an eye surgeon who runs a big private hospital. (His Eye Microsurgery Science and Technology Complex accommodates so many customers that it runs a conveyor belt of stretchers to transport an average of 1,500 patients into surgery every day, a Brave New World concept that most Americans would not countenance.)

He is, as an English language magazine in Moscow puts it, "the pied piper of capitalism." He owns an interest in the Moscow cellular telephone system that began operating in December, even as the city's infrastructure crumbled. He is helping Coca-Cola gain a stronger foothold in Russia, though he serves Pepsi (along with vodka) at his abundant dinner table. He is an owner of the Casino Royale, a fairly fancy gambling hall that offers slot machines, black jack, and roulette to possessors of hard currency, just a few blocks from the never-ending food lines. He operates clinics in 12 cities and sends mobile clinics to the Middle East to fix the eyes of oil-rich sheiks.

Fyodorov also owns a sprawling dacha where he is building a special compound for his employees. He has a fleet of Mercedes automobiles and a barn full of mechanized farm equipment. He owns a stable of horses. He is an ardent advocate of old-fashioned capitalism and believes government-owned property should be parceled out to private citizens interested in making a profit. He sees a revolt in the making that will force the development of a free-market economy and sweep out Russia's innovation-smothering bureaucracy.

"This will happen. But first the people must get a little hungrier," he says in better than passable English.

Just how Fyodorov thrived and survived as a free-market entrepreneur throughout much of the Cold War is not clear. His father, a general in the Red Army, was imprisoned for 17 years by Stalin. Fyodorov was headed for a military career himself until he lost a leg learning to be a pilot.

At a reception just before Christmas at the German-operated Penta Hotel in Moscow, Fyodorov was surrounded by apparently admiring Russian Army officers.

His close ties with military leaders, including some of his father's old comrades, may have helped him outlast the commissars who must have found his free-wheeling ways irritating.

His international reputation as an eye surgeon also gave third-world Russia worldwide prestige in medicine and science and put Fyodorov in the same class as cosmonauts: immune from banishment to Siberia.

Fyodorov, mentioned last fall as a possible prime minister for the fading USSR, may offer an opening for some Georgia businessmen to get an early foothold in Russia to capitalize on opportunities that could emerge from the current turmoil.

And it will take someone of Fyodorov's influence and stature to overcome the bureaucratic inertia to crawling out of poverty.

On his last trip to Russia in December, Miller discovered firsthand Russian reluctance to answer when opportunity knocks. He offered Russian trade officials free office space to open a Southeastern mission in Atlanta. He asked for space for Georgia officials in Moscow.

Russian officials smilingly posed for photographs with Miller, but declined to agree in writing to accept office space in Atlanta or to rent Georgia trade officials offices in Moscow.

Again, it was Fyodorov to the rescue. He would provide the Georgia trade office with space on his land near Moscow. Wayne Smith will move to Moscow for a year and represent Georgia trade interests there.

Smith Foster, a north Georgia businessman who accompanied Miller on his December trip, offered to ship a mobile home to Moscow to house the offices of the Georgia trade group.

Just how a Georgia-built double-wide might be greeted in Russia is uncertain. It could become the borscht equivalent to the Big Chicken.

"I don't care for double-wides myself, but they just might be what these people need for short-term emergency housing," says Foster, who planned to have the trailer specially built to withstand the Russian winters.

But Foster's main interest in Russia is establishing a factory to make socks. His December trip to make arrangements for the plant was his second such journey in four months. He said he had made little headway in bucking the uncertain bureaucracy and sorting out the "'tweeners," Foster's term for consultants who offer, for a handsome fee, to act as go-betweens for American businessmen and Russian government officials.

Russia seems filled with "'tweeners" these days. If they can't do business in Russia, they're ready to employ their talents elsewhere.

Isaak Tsifrin, a Russian-American who resides in California, offered to help Miller establish his lottery back in Georgia. Tsifrin said he was in Moscow to try to interest Russian officials in setting up a Russian lottery to be operated by an American company. He has had no luck so far, he said.

An Atlanta real estate speculator, who asked to remain anonymous, said he was in Moscow to acquire a tract that might be used for "the world's largest Sam's Warehouse," the discount store.

Not all "'tweeners" are the Russian equivalent of carpetbaggers and scalawags. Some appear genuinely dedicated to helping the Russians.

Besides his eye surgery deal, Smith is trying to arrange to buy tons of processed poultry in Georgia and Texas to ship to Russia to sell for a nominal price and help relieve the food shortage.

His middle man for the deal back in Georgia: former Calhoun banker and Carter administration budget director Bert Lance.

Smith also is asking his Friendship Force visitors to Russia to bring with them 100-pound food parcels to be presented to their host families.

Another Georgian, Carling Hodges of Cherokee Heating and Air Conditioning of Doraville, went to Russia to check on setting up a heating system for the Russian Orthodox Church of Nativity of Our Lady in a village near Moscow.

This was another Fyodorov-Smith endeavor. Fyodorov is restoring the ancient church that, until eight months ago, was used by the Communist government as a potato warehouse.

While Western businessmen and a few eager native hustlers mix it up, the average Russian appears sad and resigned to impoverishment.

The Baptist Church in Moscow was packed with a standing-room-only congregation on a Sunday just before Christmas. The regular service was as somber as a funeral. Not a joyful hymn was sung, and the minister never smiled. Most of the congregation were women in their 60s and 70s. Their faces reflected hopelessness.

Only a taxi driver saw a silver lining in the food lines. "That is a sign we have food here," he said. "In the other cities, there are no lines. That means there is no food."

Values and prices were without logic. Gasoline in Moscow sold for the equivalent of 10 cents a gallon on this December day; a small can of Russian black caviar sold for $35.

A traditional Russian nesting doll that costs more than $100 in the U.S. sold for less than $4.

Despite the wintry temperatures, snow, and strange language, a native American Southerner felt a sense of deja vu in post-USSR Russia.

The people and the places reminded him of the cities of the American South in the 1930s and '40s, filled with aimlessness.

Post-Communist Russia also may be a kindred soul to the post-Civil War South. Both were invaded by opportunists seeking to exploit, charitable souls hoping to bring food and hope, but mainly lands shrouded in melancholia and trepidation.

The Price of Leadership

Georgia Trend—January 1993

When Zell Miller was growing up in the Georgia mountains, "Miss Birdie," his widowed mother, advised him repeatedly: "You've got to pay for what you do." Miller never knew how right his mama was until he became governor. His list of deeds as chief executive is astonishing. But he has paid dearly for what he has done. With each new achievement, Miller's popularity has declined. As he has broken new ground and initiated new programs, he has hurt feelings and lost supporters. His accomplishments assure him a place in history. They also cast a shadow over his immediate political future.

Even so, Zell Miller was an easy choice as *Georgia Trend*'s Man of the Year. A quick review of his record shows why:

• He has accomplished more in his first two years in office than any state chief executive since Ellis Arnall in the 1940s.

• Miller performed near-miracles in the political arena. He gained passage of a state lottery that will fund improvements in education. He ended the practice of electing local school superintendents. Now, school boards can appoint qualified education administrators. He finally got a Democratic presidential candidate in the victory column in Georgia. And he rescued the candidate's national campaign from collapse early in the year.

• He guided the state through a serious recession without having to raise taxes, though he hiked a few user fees; vital services were not cut.

• He has appointed more women and blacks to the judiciary than any of his predecessors. He named the first black woman to the state Supreme Court. Miller chose the first African American to a nonjudicial constitutional office. That is how Al Scott became labor commissioner.

• Miller lassoed $50 million in excess phone-company profits from the Public Service Commission to establish a distance-learning program and a precedent-setting telemedicine network.

• He acquired 27,000 acres for park lands and recreation areas, and he plans to have 100,000 acres set aside for public use by the time he leaves office. He refocused and energized the state's economic-development programs.

That is just the beginning of what this 60-year-old overachiever—the oldest man elected governor in recent history—has accomplished in his 24 months in office. Zell Miller has drastically altered, mostly for the better, the course of Georgia's journey into the 21st century.

Yet polls show Miller has used up much of his political capital. He is in hot water with the electorate, and he might have to struggle to win the governor's office again, if he chooses to seek re-election. In a poll of business leaders attending the Georgia Chamber of Commerce's Pre-Legislative Forums in November, *Georgia Trend* found that only 37 percent thought Miller should seek re-election. While the Democratic governor performed grand governmental feats, Georgia Republicans gained unprecedented power and influence in the state's congressional delegation and Legislature. They drew much of their new-found strength from Miller's power base: North Georgia.

Fundamentalist Christians almost beat Miller's lottery initiative. They turned it into a referendum on the governor and whether he and the legislators could be trusted. The hierarchy of Miller's own United Methodist Church berated him for promoting gambling. Church leaders said he broke his word when he ran for governor on a pro-lottery platform. They said he opposed the lottery before he entered the contest.

Much of the judiciary was taken aback by his headlong rush to bring more blacks and women to the bench. Some leaders of the State Bar were stunned when Miller offered to settle a Voting Rights lawsuit by establishing racial quotas for judgeships and abandoning popular election of jurists.

Retired Supreme Court Justice George T. Smith said Miller broke a promise when he vetoed a bill that would have allowed Smith to remain on the bench past the age of 75. He replaced Smith with Leah Sears-Collins, the first black woman and youngest (36) person ever named to the court.

"Before his election, Zell Miller promised me he would support my retirement bill," Smith said. "When I asked him why he vetoed it, he just said, 'Things look different when you're governor.'"

Leaders of the Georgia House were irked when Miller blew the whistle on a secret slush fund that some lawmakers had used for political purposes. The slush fund had been in the budget for six years before Miller called attention to it. The publicity inspired Miller's House floor leader, DuBose Porter, to mount a campaign to take the House speaker's post from Miller's longtime nemesis, Thomas B. Murphy. Porter's bid failed miserably. Miller swore he had nothing to do with it, but Murphy's closest advisers believe otherwise.

The beefs against Miller are mostly minor. After all, the slush fund in the Legislature is not too different from the governor's emergency fund, except the governor's discretionary stash runs into the millions. Whether Miller had a hand in trying to toss Murphy off the speaker's throne is not important. The attempt to unseat Murphy is resulting in some overdue reform in the way the Old Boys' Club runs the House.

It's hard to make an argument that any judge, even George T. Smith, ought to be allowed to continue on the bench past 75. Besides, the court needed diversifying.

As Miller says: "Nobody is going to continue to tolerate a judiciary that does not look like the state as a whole. Nobody is going to tolerate a judiciary that is 95 percent white male. If I hadn't [diversified the courts], someone else would have."

Miller's detractors have found a rallying point that seems to distill all their antagonism against the governor in one simple symbolic issue: The governor wants to change the state flag.

He proposes removing the Confederate battle emblem from the official banner of Georgia. He believes the star-studded Confederate cross—a symbol of defiance to court-ordered integration—is offensive to many Georgians, black and white.

Non-Georgians may believe the Confederate battle flag is used mostly to decorate pickup trucks and Harley-Davidson motorcycles. But some Georgians and non-Georgians see it as an emblem of bigotry and racism.

Polls show, however, that the overwhelming majority of the state's white citizens see red when they hear Miller's words on modifying the flag that was adopted by the Legislature in 1956. Miller says Georgians are against the flag change because "many people don't understand."

"The issue doesn't have to do with whether you respect the Confederacy or anything else that happened back in the 1860s. It has to do with the fact that this—quotation marks—symbol of our state—that's what a flag is—was adopted in the most hateful, negative atmosphere that this state has seen in the last half of the 20th century," Miller declares.

"When you have a state whose motto is 'wisdom, justice and moderation,' is it wise and just and moderate to have a symbol that is hated by more than a third of our population?"

The governor says he will sponsor legislation in January to change the flag. It will almost certainly fail, and Miller knows it. "I'm going to give it my best shot, my strongest support," he declares.

It is ironic that the flag issue, perhaps the least substantive item on Miller's menu of big deeds, threatens to undermine his administration and his place in history. Miller does not even mention trying to change the flag as he ticks off a list of things for which he wishes to be remembered.

"I especially want to be remembered for what I did for Preservation 2000 (the state's acquisition and protection of public lands). I want to be remembered for what I did for education, the innovative programs ... what I did in diversifying the courts," he says.

History may remember Miller for much more. He played a decisive role in the nomination and election of Bill Clinton as president.

In late summer of 1991, he let a few friends in the media know he was interested in playing a role in national Democratic politics. In different circumstances, Miller, not Clinton, might have emerged as the "governor of a small Southern state" who would go to the White House.

When the field of Democratic contenders was finally established in late 1991, Miller supported Clinton, partly because his own two political consultants, James Carville and Paul Begala, signed on with the Arkansas governor.

In the 1992 General Assembly, Miller rammed through a bill changing Georgia's presidential primary date to March 3—a week before Super Tuesday—to give Clinton a running start at winning the big bloc of Southern states. He hit the hustings on Clinton's behalf and made it rudely clear that other Democratic contenders were not exactly welcome in Georgia.

Miller and his wife, Shirley, became close friends with Clinton's wife, Hillary. Hillary was in the Mansion with the Millers when Gennifer Flowers held a press conference to confirm reports of having a sexual liaison with Clinton.

The governor recalls Hillary endured the news with grit but did not speak disparagingly of her husband. "She is a very strong woman. The desire burned in her to see her husband win. We got up at 6:30 the next morning [to campaign for Clinton]. We were in Columbus and then in Savannah. I am one of Hillary Clinton's biggest fans. I admire her greatly."

Miller did more than admire the governor's wife. He encouraged Sen. Sam Nunn and other leading Georgia Democrats not to abandon Clinton in the face of the Flowers scandal and growing questions about his draft status. He got on the phone to Austin to admonish shaky Texas Democrats, including his pal, Gov. Ann Richards, to hold fast for Clinton. And he made certain the Georgia Democratic Party went all out for Clinton.

Clinton swept Georgia, won big on Super Tuesday and became unstoppable in his quest for the nomination. Miller was rewarded. He was chosen as a keynote speaker (one of three) at the Democratic National Convention. His speech, crafted by Clinton/Miller consultant

Paul Begala, was the hit of the convention. He slammed both President Bush and Ross Perot with old-fashioned Southern-style stump rhetoric.

"Governor Zell Miller's keynote speech was easily the most eloquent address of the opening night of the Democratic National Convention," a noted political analyst wrote.

Said Miller: "It gave me more national exposure than I ever, in my wildest dreams, thought I would have." The governor also said he believed the speech meant "people back at home would stop—as we say in the mountains—making fun of me and the way I talk." The speech did not quite stop comments on Miller's mountain twang, but it did cement his place in the history of the 1992 presidential campaign.

Miller's legislative performance at home was equally as impressive as his national maneuvering. Old-timers said Miller would never be able to persuade the people to give up popular election of local school superintendents. After all, the voters had said no, in the previous administration, to a constitutional amendment that would have abolished the elective office of state education superintendent. The old-timers were wrong.

Miller's team easily won approval of a constitutional amendment that abolished the posts of elective school supers—and the political fiefdoms that went with them. Miller had argued that professional, appointed school administrators would better serve the state's education needs. The voters apparently believed him. Still, his name went to the top of the enemies' list of nearly every elected school superintendent in the state.

When Miller was elected governor in 1990, polls showed that nearly 70 percent of Georgia residents favored a state-run lottery. By the time the lottery was put to a vote, barely half the voters favored it. The numbers-game fad was fading fast. Miller pulled the lottery issue to victory by stressing the proceeds would be used only for education, and would not replace general funds.

A big part of the lottery dollar would be used to provide free tuition to colleges and trade schools for the first two years for as many as 90,000 students from low- and middle-income families. Miller believed the rising cost of higher education had become a pressing issue in many recession-hit families who saw little hope of extending their children's education beyond high school. That promised scholarship program may have provided the margin of victory for Miller. It also gave him additional national prestige. The American Association of State Colleges and Universities presented him its 1992 award for Distinguished State Leadership in Higher Education. *City & State* magazine chose Miller as its Most Valuable Public Official in state government for 1992.

In the area of economic development, Miller created the Georgia Research Alliance to promote cooperation in high-tech research among six universities. In time, it may outshine North Carolina's Research Triangle, Miller hopes. The governor ordered the state's industry-recruiting efforts directed away from low-cost, labor-intensive endeavors and toward upscale corporations that will require a much better-educated labor force than Georgia now offers.

Strangely, Miller's record romp with his initiatives through the Legislature of 1992 received relatively minor attention. The media were focused on legislative ethics and reapportionment. The governor played virtually no role in decisions on either topic.

He also encountered a couple of bumps in the road. He attempted to establish a state Bond Bank to facilitate borrowing by local governments at improved interest rates. The proposal was shot down by bond attorneys who contended the idea was little more than a way for Miller to reward bond-lawyer Ed Sims, Miller's personal financial adviser and chairman of the state Democratic Party. Sims and Miller, of course, denied such was the case.

The governor set out to establish a super-chief position in the Public Safety Department. He wanted passage of a law that would create a single administrative director of the GBI, State Patrol, and other state law-enforcement agencies. He would appoint then-DeKalb District Attorney Bob Wilson to the post. The Legislature, particularly the House, wouldn't hear of it. Wilson was too close to Attorney General Mike Bowers, and Bowers is to House Speaker Tom Murphy what Arafat is to Israel.

Even so, Speaker Murphy has had high praise for Miller, with whom he has feuded off and on for 25 years. "That is the best speech I have ever heard a Democrat make," Murphy said last year of the governor's standard stump speech on bringing the Democratic Party to the center of the political spectrum.

Murphy's praise may not be so lavish in the upcoming legislative session. He says Miller's budget forecast is far too optimistic. "I believe we are heading for a $200 million shortfall," Murphy says. "I hope I am wrong."

A clash over the budget is nearly a certainty in the 1993 Legislature. Miller also may choose to endorse a recommendation from a blue-ribbon study panel that would reduce the number of local governments in the state. If he does, that will stir a mighty fuss. Some tinkering with the lottery law is bound to be proposed, and Miller will resist. Then there's the flag issue, of course.

When a reporter asks what new major initiatives Miller has in mind for the final two years of this administration, the governor lapses into quoting Ecclesiastes: "To every thing there is a season, and a time to every purpose under the heaven."

What does that mean?

Miller: "There's a time for everything. There's a time for being very, very proactive and getting all these things out there. There's a time for consolidating your gains and making things work."

In other words, don't look for any major new initiatives, right, governor?

Miller: "Well, I wouldn't say that."

Each of Georgia's governors since World War II has made significant contributions to bringing once-impoverished Georgia into the national mainstream. Ellis Arnall gave the state a modern constitution, prison reform, and freight rates equal to the rest of the nation. He wrote the de facto end to Reconstruction.

Herman Talmadge enacted the 3-percent sales tax that allowed Georgia to spend more on schools and transportation.

Marvin Griffin accelerated highway building and the rural-roads program.

Ernest Vandiver preserved public education and instituted major reform in the state's scandal-ridden mental health system.

Carl Sanders enhanced higher education and integrated state government.

Lester Maddox instituted a humane parole and prisons system.

Jimmy Carter reorganized and streamlined state government.

George Busbee made unprecedented strides in economic development and created a statewide network of kindergartens.

Joe Frank Harris gained approval of a Quality Basic Education program.

Now comes Miller. After he has finished, what would he have posterity list as his one-line contribution?

"I have lived my entire adult life, my life in politics, wanting to get into this office to actively improve education," he says.

"That has been my strongest desire. I would always flinch when I read that Georgia was last in the nation in this, and last in that. I always dreamed of becoming governor and correcting that.

"If we had not had a recession, I would have been more active. I wish we could have had the revenue to take the sales tax off food. I would certainly have done that."

Despite repeated denials, reports persist that Miller may leave the governor's office to accept an appointment in the Clinton administration.

"Absolutely not," he says. "I like this job very much. I like being governor. I like the challenge of trying to make things work. I like trying to put this opposing faction with that opposing faction and putting a coalition together. Even in the darkest days of the recession, I never got up without really looking forward to coming to work."

Even if Miller's popularity at midterm is in a valley, only a daring challenger would take him on in 1994. Republicans are aware they could give the governor grief with a popular and well-known conservative candidate. They also know Miller is well-armed for any election battle. His incumbency ensures he will have a fat campaign treasury and probably no primary opposition. He has at his disposal the most talented Democratic consultants in the land: James Carville and Paul Begala. He has the full support of the still-dominant state Democratic hierarchy, and he has easy entree to the Bill Clinton White House with all the advantages that implies. Those active assets keep even the most confident Republicans wondering if 1998 might not be a better year to stand for governor, when Miller surely will be bowing out of the political picture.

Still, Miller won't say yes when asked if he plans a second term. "I haven't made up my mind," he says, and he won't reveal whom he might support if he decides to quit. He seems to lean toward helping Lt. Gov. Pierre Howard.

"At this particular point in history, [Howard] is the strongest lieutenant governor I have ever seen," says Miller, who served as lieutenant governor for 16 years.

The governor is stoic about the increasing criticism of his administration. He show no inclination to change course to reduce the carping. "You know why I am governor?' he asks rhetorically. "It is not because I am so smart or so sensitive or anything like that. It is because I have persevered. I never gave up. I was beaten twice for Congress and once for the Senate, and I came back. Not many politicians have done that. Every time they wrote my obituary, I got up and came back."

And he apparently plans to keep on coming back.

In 1997, Miller turned down two invitations from President Bill Clinton, one to run for the Senate in 1998, the other to become director of a national scholarship program.

Two Aging Lions

Syndicated column—February 27, 1994

House Speaker Tom Murphy railed against his enemies and wept publicly from the well of the House.

Gov. Zell Miller sat quietly in his office as he marked his 62nd birthday. He posed for pictures with school children, then went to lunch with a handful of old friends from the state Senate.

It was a week that provided a study in contrasts of the two most influential figures in Georgia government, both of whom may be approaching their final political battles.

Murphy, who will be 70 on March 12, is angry with his House of Representatives, over which he is steadily losing control. He is so steamed up against his detractors that he exudes exasperation and frustration in making even the most routine rulings from the speaker's podium.

Miller seems almost relaxed, resigned to a coming re-election campaign that many believe will be among the bitterest and most expensive in Georgia history.

Voter-registration projections suggest suburban Republicans will shortly hold the balance of power in the state. Three heavily Republican counties in metro Atlanta—Cherokee, Cobb, and Gwinnett—are expected to turn out at least 100,000 voters more than in 1990. Republican suburbs in other sections of the state are reporting equally dramatic increases in voter registration.

At the same time, African-American enthusiasm for the Democratic powers is on the wane. In 1990, black voters cheered on Andy Young in the Democratic primary, then turned out in near-record numbers for Miller in the general election.

They are not likely to follow that pattern this year. Miller's failed attempt to change the state flag, his insistence on welfare reform, and his demand for tougher criminal penalties have cooled black enthusiasm for his governorship. He cannot win re-election without a substantial black vote; he is far short of having a majority of whites on his side.

Miller is in deep trouble, and he knows it. Yet, he doesn't show it. He is busy raising money and preparing to defend his record in office.

His would-be challengers—Guy Millner, Paul Heard, John Knox, and Nimrod McNair—are even more engaged in getting ready for a GOP primary that each is certain will produce the next Georgia governor.

It has not quite dawned on them that Miller is a determined and mean fighter, a politician with a plan who will not go quietly.

By comparison, Murphy and his men apparently have developed no strategy for hanging on to their power base. They are simply thrashing about, trying to punish their perceived enemies with insults and ostracism.

When Reform Democrat Leader Ken Poston attempted to gain passage of a bill to help disabled persons, a Murphy lieutenant publicly told supporters of the bill that Rep. Poston is "your greatest handicap."

When a radio talk-show host criticized the speaker, Murphy resorted to crying from the podium—a tactic he has used several times in his 20-year career as speaker—and threatened to "beat the brains out of" the radio announcer.

On any significant issue this year, Murphy can be certain to draw at least 50 Republican votes against him and another dozen from dissenting Democrats in the 180-member House. That number of "nays" is bound to grow significantly after the next election.

There is an even more telling sign that Murphy is slipping. The "rail birds"—the lobbyists who pilot the most significant bills through the Legislature—are turning increasingly to the Senate as a starting place for their proposals.

"Five years ago, the speaker could tell you with certainty how well a bill might play in the House, how many votes it would get, and whether it would pass. He can't do that any longer—because he doesn't know," says a veteran wheeler-dealer in the Capitol. "It's safer now to start a bill in the Senate. The process is more orderly. The lieutenant governor (Pierre Howard) is more in control than the speaker."

In any event, the two aging lions of Georgia politics, Miller and Murphy, who began their climb to power 30 years ago, are facing the sternest tests of their careers in the coming elections.

Miller won re-election against multimillionaire Guy Millner. Murphy remained speaker, but Republicans made significant gains in the General Assembly in the election of 1994.

Carter to The Rescue

Syndicated column — June 22, 1994

Jimmy Carter may have saved us from a great war in Asia, but you don't hear much cheering from the White House for the ex-president.

Carter went to Korea last week, arranged an unprecedented summit meeting between the leaders of North and South Korea, and gave North Korea's Kim Il Sung a face-saving way out of a confrontation with South Korea and the United States.

Carter probably engaged in his bad old habit of stating the situation not precisely as it is, but as he wishes it were. He said yessiree, the U.S. and the U.N. would put aside sanctions against North Korea, and the U.S. might even provide aid to North Korea in developing nuclear power for peaceful uses.

The White House was not entirely happy. Carter sort of misspoke, said a spokesperson for President Clinton. If there was not a resounding round of applause for Carter, there should have been.

Korea is not Somalia or Haiti or some other backwater. Korea is potentially mushroom cloud-size trouble, and so is its Asian neighbor, China.

The Koreas have been ticking time bombs since they were divided in 1945. The Korean War of the early 1950s came close to triggering an Asia-wide confrontation that might still be going on had not cooler heads in Washington scotched cries to expand the hostilities into China.

Of all the problems the overachiever from Plains has tackled since the voters booted him from the Oval Office, his mission to Korea may have been the most significant.

President Clinton could take credit for allowing Carter to go to Asia to defuse the coming crisis. After all, the president needs a foreign-policy victory. He also might use Carter a bit more for keeping his presidency better focused. That is not likely.

The truth is, Carter and Clinton are allies of convenience. Both are Southerners and former governors. And both are infected with Politician's Syndrome, the desperate need to be loved and praised by everyone for every deed, every minute of the day and night. The similarities end there.

Carter was the son of a country squire, a prosperous farmer, merchant, and politician. Clinton grew up on the wrong side of the tracks among poor whites who were always scrambling to survive. As any Southerner can tell you, the gulf between those two classes of whites is wider than even the differences between the races.

When Clinton was defeated for governor of Arkansas in 1980, he laid part of the blame on President Carter. He said Carter's decision to locate Cuban refugees, many of them criminals and mentally ill, in Arkansas cost him thousands of Democratic votes. Years later, Carter's aides grumbled that Clinton was a whiner of whom they were not particularly fond.

Carter put aside old grievances in 1992 and, at the behest of Gov. Zell Miller and other Democratic leaders, heartily endorsed Clinton for president.

Now Carter seems to have delivered him — and the rest of us — from a particularly dangerous situation.

When the history of the 20th century is written, Jimmy Carter will certainly turn out to be among the most important public figures Georgia and the South have produced. He also may be one of the most complicated.

He campaigned for governor as a racist, which he was not. (He has since ordered sealed his records of his 1970 gubernatorial campaign.) He was a moderate governor who spent much of his tenure planning a campaign for the White House. He set a tone of needed restraint for his Statehouse successors.

In retrospect, his presidency ushered in a remarkable era of peace and prosperity, although Carter was hounded by bad luck and bad press.

A statue of Carter was recently unveiled on the state Capitol lawn. In a way, it is a perfect symbol of the former president. It depicts an unsmiling Carter in workman's clothing. It apparently shows Carter in the way he wants the public to perceive him. It is not quite the Carter many of us know and remember.

Tom Murphy: An Unchanged Icon from the '70s

Syndicated column—December 14, 1994

Richard Nixon resigned, and President Gerald Ford granted Nixon a pardon.

In Georgia, Zell Miller mounted a campaign for lieutenant governor. Lt. Gov. Lester Maddox presided over the state Senate. Gov. Jimmy Carter told incredulous supporters he hoped to run for president. (President of what? they asked.) Newt Gingrich, a 31-year-old assistant professor at West Georgia College, made his first bid for a seat in Congress. He lost.

Rural Democrats dominated Georgia government and the General Assembly. Not a single constitutional officer, except Maddox, came from the Atlanta area. Only a handful of Republicans held legislative seats.

It was 1974. State Rep. Tom Murphy, a querulous country lawyer from Bremen, became speaker of the Georgia House.

Now, two decades later, Nixon is dead, and Ford is still working on his golf game. Miller is governor. Maddox is retired. Carter is an elder statesman who claims to be a poet. Gingrich has gained international fame, and will soon become speaker of the U.S. House.

Georgia government is controlled by suburbia. Not one constitutional officer comes from south of Macon. Georgia has elected four Republicans to statewide offices and one to the U.S. Senate. Seven of our U.S. representatives are Republicans, and there are 87 members of the GOP (66 representatives and 21 senators) in the 256-member Legislature.

Tom Murphy, the last of the wool-hat Democrats, remains speaker of the Georgia House. He is about the only item in the state that hasn't changed much in the past two decades.

For most of his tenure, Murphy has presided with an iron fist. Dissident Democrats were shut out of power. Republicans were ignored, women patronized. Selected lobbyists were welcome, the others were shut out. Murphy promulgated rules of secrecy and fought any attempt to give the public more access to the doings of the Legislature.

Yet he has maintained an atmosphere of stability and moderation, until now.

Suddenly, the speaker finds himself on the edge of a full-fledged rebellion in the House. A handful of disaffected Democrats believe he is out of touch with the times. Republicans are gathering to block his every attempt to exercise power.

The GOP, with the help of alienated Democrats, finally has an opportunity to seize the last power post occupied by a rural Democrat.

Even so, Murphy is an odds-on favorite to be elected to at least one more two-year term before the suburban tidal wave washes away the last traces of courthouse-based Democratic power.

Fortunately for Murphy and the few surviving Democratic officeholders, Georgia Republicans in 1994 remain divided and inept. Their confusion and intraparty squabbling almost assure Murphy's continued reign.

Their recent governor's race was a masterpiece of bungled opportunity.

They can't get their act together for a unified campaign in the Georgia House. The 66 House Republicans are divided roughly among three warring factions.

House Minority Leader Bob Irvin of North Fulton leads one group, which seems to have little stomach for tackling Murphy. Ultraconservative Reps. Mitchell Kaye of Marietta and Scott Dix of Snellville are prepared for an all-out battle to wrest control from Murphy. But they want no part of a Democratic coalition or a Democratic candidate for speaker.

And three or four Republicans only give lip service to GOP goals, while they continue to cozy up to Murphy.

The aging Democrat can't count on the Republican disarray lasting forever, or even two more years.

Murphy has around him three or four able lieutenants who could pick up his mantle and maintain a stable and progressive House agenda. Yet, the speaker refuses to hand off power.

In two years, he will be dumped, and his loyal would-be successors will be booted along with him. They will be replaced by men determined to rip away and make over everything Murphy believes he has accomplished.

What do I know? Murphy was easily re-elected speaker of the Georgia House in 1996.

The Rage against Newt

Syndicated column—August 16, 1995

The incessant vilification of Newt Gingrich is unnerving.

What is there about the speaker of the House that inspires such outrage?

No member of the Congress since Sen. Joe McCarthy has been subjected to such condemnation by the media and his Washington colleagues. In McCarthy's case, however, the press and the political establishment gave the Communist-hunting senator wide berth until alcoholism and the conduct of his sleazy aides had all but finished him.

Such is not the case with Gingrich. The speaker is at the peak of his power and growing in stature.

The rage against him has become almost deafening. He cannot appear at a public forum to explain his views without being shouted down by his adversaries.

In Atlanta, 5th District Rep. John Lewis, D-Atlanta, showed up in support of a rowdy rally to shut off Gingrich's discourse on Medicare and welfare reform.

Of all people, Lewis, a battered veteran of the civil rights wars, should know what it means to be told by a mob to sit down and shut up.

In Denver, militant liberal Rep. Pat Schroeder inspired an equally boisterous protest against the Marietta lawmaker when he made an appearance to sign his book, *To Renew America.*

Vanity Fair, the upscale gossip magazine, published a 12,000-word psycho-profile of Gingrich that painted him as a wild-eyed nut and exploited 19-year-old allegations of marital infidelity.

The magazine story was front-page news in Washington and New York.

A national television show, "TV Nation," focused on Gingrich and Cobb County, implying the speaker poured millions of federal dollars into the county while he argued against government spending. Producers of the show failed to mention Gingrich only moved to Cobb County three years ago.

Besides, as a member of the minority party until the elections of 1994, Gingrich had minimal influence on federal spending. Cobb's largesse flowed mostly from Democrats.

The media have pilloried Gingrich almost from the day of his election in 1994.

A CBS news anchor, Connie Chung, tricked his mother into making a disparaging remark about Hillary Clinton. *The Washington Post, The New York Times,* and even *The New York Post,* owned by Gingrich's benefactor Rupert Murdoch, have taken turns slamming Gingrich, often in personal terms.

A noted *Wall Street Journal* columnist has hinted darkly that investigators will drop a headline-making bombshell on Gingrich if he doesn't change his views. (Blackmail, anyone?)

Teams of investigative reporters have spent days in Georgia and his home state, Pennsylvania, looking for any sliver of information that could discredit him.

Gingrich must possess the most accurate curriculum vitae and financial statement on the planet. Every line in each document has been checked and double-checked for the slightest imprecision.

The media have turned into bulls. Newt is a red cloth. This is strange behavior indeed, because Gingrich, of all national figures, has been accessible to the press. Gingrich seemed to enjoy give-and-take with journalists, until their questions focused more on his id than his intellect.

To be sure, Gingrich is fair game. His adversary, former Congressman Ben Jones, has filed charges against him in the House Ethics Committee, and that panel has taken an inordinate amount of time in dealing with the accusations.

It is the kind of thing that would have made the old Newt fume, which he did in 1988 when Democrats dawdled over a similar investigation into then-Speaker Jim Wright's book deal. Gingrich wrote: "The House of Representatives, as well as the American public, deserves an investigation which will uncover the truth. At the moment, I am afraid that the apparent restrictions ... will not allow the truth to be uncovered."

That is tepid rhetoric compared to today's red-hot verbal blasts at Gingrich. The speaker advocates sweeping changes, some of which may not be in the nation's best interest over the long haul. His detractors should turn down the volume so we can decide for ourselves. Their current personalized assault on Gingrich leads one to believe they are afraid we will hear him out.

Young to Bowers: Keep Quiet About Crime

Syndicated column—April 3, 1996

The following episode would be nearly humorous if it did not deal with such a serious topic.

Andrew Young, who built his reputation as an outspoken boat-rocker, has told a present-day boat-rocker to pipe down.

The former U.N. ambassador, U.S. congressman, and Atlanta mayor has informed Attorney General Michael Bowers that his recent assertions about crime in Atlanta were "certainly ill-timed and harmful to our efforts to present Atlanta as a city of the 21st century."

You may recall that Bowers made national headlines when he suggested Atlanta is more dangerous than Sarajevo and produced a bushel of statistics on violent crime to prove it. Everybody from Atlanta Mayor Bill Campbell to the state Democratic Party jumped on Bowers for talking too much about Atlanta's dirty linen. Now Young has chimed in.

"Dear Michael. ... Georgia's growth is fueled by what happens in Atlanta, so we would ask restraint," the 1960s civil rights marcher/preacher wrote Bowers. Young, of course, is no longer on the outside looking in, no longer Young the Dreaded Activist of the 1960s but Andy the Venerated Village Elder of the 1990s.

He is a part of the Establishment he once attacked, and image-protecting is his job. As mayor, he was as good a booster and salesman as the city has ever had. He deserves much credit for bringing the Olympic Games to Atlanta. He is now chairman of the Atlanta Chamber of Commerce.

It is difficult to determine why Young felt inspired to chastise Bowers.

Did the reverend's impending marriage flaw his judgment?

Or did he feel Bowers needed a political boost and he wanted to make certain the AG is elevated to governor in a couple of years?

Whatever his motive, Young's March 20 letter will become an important part of Bowers' future campaigns for elective office. Imagine being attacked by Andrew Young for speaking out against crime. For a Republican, that is better than receiving a million dollars worth of

85

prime TV time or having Bill & Hillary campaign against you. The AG reportedly has been reluctant to display the Young letter. He must know the document will make him the envy of every aspiring GOP pol in the state.

Bowers' reply to Young's request for restraint is an old-fashioned mad-as-hell piece of defiance.

"Perhaps one reason we have the level of criminal activity in Atlanta, the State of Georgia, and the rest of the nation is that there has been too much restraint in discussing and confronting the reality of crime. I understand the desire to depict Atlanta as a safe and attractive site for the 1996 Olympics, but the fact of the matter is that comparatively, Atlanta, and other urban areas in the United States, are more dangerous than much of the rest of the world," Bowers wrote on March 28.

"When I no longer have reason to be concerned for the safety of the employees of the Department of Law as they walk to their cars at night not two blocks from City Hall and the state Capitol, I will have reason for restraint. When secretaries from my office can eat lunch in Underground Atlanta without being accosted and touched by unwanted hands, I will have reason for restraint. When the carjackings, robberies, murders, drug dealings, and gang activities cease, I will exercise restraint. But to do so now would be a failure on my part to be honest with the public and myself," Bowers wrote. "Thank you for your letter and your continued concern over the welfare of our city and our state."

Next time, Andy, consider a friendly phone call. Recent incidents of highly publicized crime suggest Bowers was on target. His words are turning out to be more prophetic than alarmist.

SECTION III

POLITICS

Possum Recipe Tricky

Atlanta Journal-Constitution - November 1970

When you gourmets have polished off the turkey and dressing on this Turkey Day, you can look forward to Dec. 6—Possum Day, as proclaimed by Gov. Lester Maddox.

That's the second day of what is billed as the "World's Largest Possum Hunt" in the north Georgia mountains around Dillard.

Dec. 6 also is the proper day to eat possum, which is described as "a real delicacy" in the governor's fancy proclamation that pays tribute to "the small primitive American animals ... related to the kangaroo ... and plentiful in the state of Georgia."

There are a number of ways to cook possum, such as roasted with potatoes. But Maddox's executive secretary, Zell Miller, described by one reliable source as the governor's closest adviser on matters relating to possums, has come up with a recipe for possum stew that requires one medium-sized flint rock. The possum stew recipe goes like this:

1/4 lb. bacon diced
1 cup chopped onion
1/4 lb. mushrooms, sliced
1 medium-sized possum, cut up
3 teaspoons butter or margarine
1 bay leaf
1/2 teaspoon tarragon, crumbled
4 peppercorns
10 sprigs of parsley
1 teaspoon salt
1 teaspoon flour
2 teaspoons chopped parsley
1 medium-sized flint rock

Cook bacon in skillet until brown and crispy; remove and reserve bacon. Cook onion and mushrooms until soft in hot bacon fat; remove and reserve. Wash and dry possum. Add three tablespoons butter or margarine to bacon fat in skillet; add possum and brown. Return bacon, onion, and mushrooms to skillet.

Tie bay leaf, tarragon, peppercorns, and parsley in small piece of clean cloth and add to skillet. Add salt. Place flint rock in skillet.

Simmer with cover on for about 25 minutes or until possum is tender. Remove the cloth and herbs. Blend flour and tablespoon of butter together; add to hot liquid bit by bit. Remove flint rock (which is supposed to get rid of the wild taste).

Miller guarantees this is delicious. But one of his mountaineer friends says he knows of an even better version of the above recipe: "Throw away the possum and eat the rock." Obviously not a possum eater.

Barf!

How to Prepare Crow, Etc.

Atlanta Journal-Constitution — August 28, 1980

As a public service to the relatively small number of our fellow Georgians who believed it was time to un-elect Herman Talmadge and who may now feel the time has come to eat crow, we offer the following recipe eagerly provided by Georgia Natural Resources Commissioner Joe Tanner:

BARBECUED CROW: Split whole crow in half and flatten with side of cleaver. Place on a rack in a baking pan and cook at 375 degrees F for 45 minutes. Baste every 10 minutes with sauce. Turn on the other side for 30 minutes.

SAUCE FOR BARBECUED CROW:
One-half teaspoon butter
One-half cup ketchup
1 teaspoon sugar
One and one-half teaspoons lemon juice
1 teaspoon Worcestershire sauce
Ground black pepper
1 tablespoon salt
1 clove pressed garlic
1 chopped small onion
One and one-half teaspoons Tabasco
Combine all ingredients and simmer for five minutes.

(The state Department of Natural Resources heartily recommends two stiff drinks of good bourbon before biting into this delicacy.)

Perhaps we should offer Sen. Talmadge our gratitude for a learning experience. He taught us something we did not know or perhaps had forgotten. Namely, given the choice of a liberal or anything else, Georgia voters will select the anything else every time.

Nearly 60 percent of the Georgia voters showed that they cared not a whit that Talmadge played fast and loose with their money and that his colleagues in the Senate thought his conduct disgraceful. You could say Talmadge's conduct was embarrassing, but you could never say it was liberal.

Great numbers of black voters in south Georgia cast ballots for Talmadge. No matter that he was the father of a white primary bill that would have prevented them from voting in this primary, if it had stood. No matter that he opposed civil rights legislation throughout his career. In their eyes he had atoned for all that.

Herman's daddy, Gene, would not have been surprised. Gene didn't get much help where the streetcars ran. And Talmadge's opponent, Zell Miller, walloped the old boy mostly where MARTA runs—in Fulton and DeKalb counties.

Talmadge spent more, $6 to Miller's every $1, on the campaign. He poured more dollars into winning a Georgia primary than any candidate in history.

Miller, unfortunately, aided and abetted the Talmadge effort. He let Talmadge tie a liberal tag around his neck, and it stayed. He allowed Talmadge to select the time and place of the television debates and lay down the rules. He relied on Maynard Jackson and Julian Bond to bring out the black vote for Miller. Instead, they succeeded in turning out the white vote for Talmadge.

Talmadge had all the fat cats in his corner who were either glad-handing would-be supporters or trying to browbeat opponents.

In fact, Talmadge had it all—money, power, resources. Miller had a rag-tag coalition of liberals, labor, and urban blacks—the kind of people who can get you only one thing in politics in this state: beat.

Talmadge's opponents now should forgive and forget and perhaps pitch in and buy the old boy a peace offering that could last him for the next six years. How about a brand-new overcoat with bigger-than-ever pockets?

Now we shall see what Herman can do against one Mack Mattingly, who is neither a liberal nor anything else but a Ronald Reagan-style Republican who is the darling of the Moral Majority. Wonder what Scriptures Talmadge will quote to try to throw him off guard.

Mack Mattingly defeated Herman Talmadge in the general election of 1980.

The Road Not Taken

Atlanta Magazine — December 1989

The rain fell in glistening, almost opaque sheets along U.S. Highway 29 on a football Saturday afternoon. Cars and vans, their red-and-black pennants drenched and drooping, lined up inches apart, stop-go-stop-go-stop-go, from Athens to the Atlanta cutoff west of Dacula. Thousands crept in their vehicles toward home, to leave the defeated Georgia Bulldogs licking their wounds and to get on with their separate weekends.

Bored by the whump-whump-whump of the windshield wipers and the whimpering self-flagellation of a rookie head coach on the radio, my brain scanned a mental directory of a hundred barely connected topics. I glanced through the rain streaks on the side window at a historical plaque beside the highway just outside the town of Winder. It marked in a golden-lettered caption the home and burial site of the late Sen. Richard B. Russell. Richard Brevard Russell Jr. might have been president, except he was born in the wrong region at the wrong time and espoused the wrong philosophy.

Nonetheless, he was a man of vast influence. He died in 1971.

The plaque went out of sight in the rain, and the pages of my mind flipped to other subjects: numbers, mangled bodies and the wet road ahead. How many unfortunate college kids and other travelers have met death or permanent impairment in car crashes on this miserable little highway in the last 30 years?

And why are the capital city of the Southeast and the learning center of the state connected only by a set of traffic-choked, dangerous, barely improved pig paths instead of by a safe, limited-access interstate highway?

Why are we just now getting around to widening roads that connect what are, arguably, the two most important locales in Georgia?

Sadly, I know some of the reasons. Athens and the University of Georgia were passed over for an interstate highway route because of greed. No, make that "more influence" elsewhere. I remember when and how it happened. The decision didn't seem important or even newsworthy at the time.

Civil-rights protests and mental-health scandals were the significant stories then, back there in the late 1950s and early '60s. Choosing highway routes was better left to engineers, or so we thought. As it turned out, it was engineers' work all right. Except, in the end, the engineers were told to step aside. The politicians drew the highway maps and put the concrete and asphalt where their personal interests dictated instead of where traffic counts and logic prescribed. Then they called back the engineers and told them to make it look justifiable.

An old friend, now a state pensioner, recently remembered and briefly recounted the story of locating Interstate 85 in northeast Georgia. It is a tale that signifies more about our style of governance than all the political science courses you will ever take. The old friend, for understandable reasons, asks that his name be omitted from this saga.

A lasting contribution of the administration of President Dwight D. Eisenhower was the interstate highway system that was born by act of Congress in 1956. It changed the face of our nation more dramatically than any other interior alteration since the advent of railroads.

Drowsy hamlets sprang to life when they were touched by the interstates. Likewise, live-wire towns, brought into being years ago by the arrival of the trains, withered when they were bypassed by the interstate mappers.

In Washington, transportation engineers pored over charts and decreed that Atlanta, already an air and rail transportation hub with the beginnings of a four-lane expressway system, was a natural universal joint for the interstate network. Interstates 75, 85, and 20 would intersect there.

But how would the tentacles of the interstate system be shaped as they reached out from Atlanta?

Picking the route for Interstate 85 northeast of Atlanta seemed simple enough. There were two logical paths—one taking in Athens, the other Gainesville—that could guide the great autobahn across the Georgia piedmont into the Carolinas and up the East Coast. Those were the only two courses that made sense. At least that's what the federal highway-route designers first thought—before they were informed of "local political considerations."

Justifying a route for the interstate highway that would touch bustling Gainesville would be a piece of pie. The interstate could serve to facilitate the fledgling poultry and established textile industries around that northeast Georgia trade center. Gainesville, in no time, could become another Macon or even Charlotte with the help of a direct interstate highway route. Besides, the Gainesville path would open up Georgia's impoverished and isolated mountain region.

The other option: Athens. The University of Georgia town was just beginning to shake off its cow-college image and emerge as one of the economic and educational hot spots of the South. Joining Atlanta (home of Georgia Tech and the forerunner institution of Georgia State University) with Athens was a natural matchup. Easy access between Atlanta and Athens would form a research-education axis between the two cities and could create a linear city extending 60 miles across the foothills of the northeast Georgia mountains.

Gainesville and Athens — those were the two alternatives suggested by federal engineers as the most propitious routes for Interstate 85. Except they forgot the middle route. They ignored Lavonia and a governor from Lavonia named S. Ernest Vandiver and the powerful United States senator whose home and grave are marked alongside U.S. 29. Dick Russell happened to be Ernie Vandiver's uncle by marriage. They were a close-knit clan.

If Interstate 85 went by way of Athens, U.S. 29 would become a deserted byway. Winder, Russell's beloved hometown, would likely dry up. But surely such selfish considerations would not be taken into account in placing a highway that could bring such benefit to Georgia.

If Interstate 85 went by way of Athens or Gainesville, it also would bypass Lavonia. Lavonia? So what? The governor owned some property there. It was a nice little town but not exactly the potential economic pump of an Athens or Gainesville.

Enter our "old friend," now a slightly cynical and much older consultant for a fat conglomerate. Then, he was a young and ambitious fellow who could be trusted by the powers that were, powers named Russell and Vandiver. As a bright state highway engineer with a keen and inventive mind, he was given the assignment of making "the Lavonia option" more economically attractive than either the Athens or Gainesville plan.

The job was better suited to a creative-writing graduate from the English department at Georgia than a product of Tech's engineering school. But our anonymous friend did as he was told. He pondered the problem, then simply drew the impact area of Interstate Highway 85 through Lavonia so wide (more than 50 miles wide, in fact) that it encompassed both Athens and Gainesville. Thus, the Lavonia corridor included, on paper, all the advantages of both other routes.

With "Uncle Dick" Russell and his staff looking over their shoulders, the feds in Washington agreed quickly and eagerly there was no doubt that the Lavonia way was most feasible. After all, it enveloped all the attributes of both Athens and Gainesville plus the wonders of Lavonia (pop. 2,088 in 1960). So the way was cleared for

Interstate 85 to strike out through the not-exactly-teeming podunks of Braselton and Commerce and right on through Lavonia.

Thirty years later, Athens continues to gag on traffic. The drive between Atlanta and the mistitled Classic City is always an ordeal and sometimes a nightmare.

Gainesville, shunted to the side of I-85, is just now coming into its own. Think what it might have been had the main interstate highway, instead of a split-off road, crossed the Gainesville dot on the map in the early 1960s.

Ernie Vandiver is remembered as one of the good-guy governors. Even if he did fudge a little with Interstate 85, that was small-time stuff compared to the asphalt shenanigans of some of his contemporaries. (One of these days, we'll tell you about Gov.-then-Sen. Herman Talmadge and I-75.)

And Russell? No one thinks of him in the parochial terms of protecting Winder and saving U.S. 29 from the ravages of progress. He is remembered as a presidential candidate, president *pro tempore* of the United States Senate, a champion of a strong national defense, a close pal of Lyndon Johnson, and the man who helped inspire the kind of leadership for which the South is noted today.

On Honoring Living and Dead Politicians

Syndicated column—November 25, 1990

Taking the most direct route from Atlanta to Phil Landrum's house in Jasper, you must drive up the Zell Miller Appalachian Highway.

Landrum, one of the political giants from Georgia's post–World War II era, died last week. More than anyone else, retired 9th District Rep. Landrum steered millions of federal dollars into his beloved mountain region. He got the money for the Zell Miller highway. Miller tried twice to beat Landrum for Congress.

Landrum saw to it that U.S. funds were provided for other roads, schools and even water- and sewage-treatment plants in the mountains.

If you're a newcomer to Georgia, you may know the name Landrum best as part of the title of the Landrum-Griffin Act, the last significant federal law that imposed restrictions on labor unions.

Yet Landrum's achievements transcend his co-authorship of the Landrum-Griffin Act. He was among the first Southerners in Congress to oppose the Vietnam War. He questioned the findings of the Warren Commission on the assassination of President Kennedy.

He was Lyndon Johnson's point man in the House for the war on poverty. Landrum was a moving force behind the establishment of the Appalachian Commission.

"Someone should build a monument to Phil Landrum," President Johnson said when he came to Georgia in 1964 to help Landrum fight off a challenge by Miller.

They built a monument to Miller instead and named the nearby highway in honor of this living, active politician who will shortly become governor of the state. (In fairness, it ought to be reported that Landrum and his protege, 9th District Rep. Ed Jenkins, supported Miller for governor in the last election.)

Not only has a highway been named for Miller, but an auditorium in the World Congress Center bears his name. And who has not heard of the Thomas B. Murphy Ballroom in the World Congress Center named in honor of the current speaker of the Georgia House? Or the

Tom Moreland Interchange on I-85 named for the former transportation commissioner, still active in behind-the-scenes politics at age 57?

Now we have a new statue erected on Capitol Square honoring former Sen. Herman E. Talmadge, who attended its unveiling.

But nowhere on the Capitol grounds will you find a statue of Landrum or even of Walter F. George, possibly the most influential senator Georgia ever produced.

Except for a pale portrait in the Capitol, there is not much recognition that Ellis Gibbs Arnall ever passed this way. As governor in the 1940s, he began pulling Georgia away from the politics of racism that had stunted its growth for a century.

Still, we continue to name enduring edifices in honor of living politicians. To be certain, Zell Miller and Tom Murphy and the energetic pals of Talmadge can be more helpful in the appropriations process than the late Sen. George or Rep. Landrum or the ailing and aging Gov. Arnall. So supplicants, eager to please the current powers, naturally offer to name all sorts of things for the Murphys, Millers, and even Talmadges.

Perhaps Miller, a historian by profession, will finally note the unseemliness of this practice.

Most of the tasks facing the new governor will require millions, even billions of dollars to fix.

Getting the state's historical priorities in order should cost little, if anything.

Establishing a nonpartisan commission to decide qualifications for future political memorials on Capitol Square and other state property might be in order. A law banning the naming of any buildings, ballrooms, bridges or ballparks for living politicians might be worth passing, too.

Miller could set a precedent by ordering the removal of the markers bearing his name from alongside the highway started by the man he tried to depose from Congress. He might even want to change its name to the Phil Landrum Appalachian Highway.

Now It's Miller Time

Atlanta Magazine — January 1991

A letter to our old pal, Zell Miller, soon-to-be 79th governor of Georgia:

Dear Zell,

A dozen years have gone by since a bunch of us, including you, were sitting around The Little Mug one night, commiserating about the state of the state. I wonder if you remember. We grumbled about the threadbare quality of our elected leadership. We said it was a real shame to have such a great state run by such a scraggly gang of nincompoops.

Somebody in the crowd who obviously had put too many crackers in his soup shouted: "Why, hell, Zell, you could do something about it, if you just had the balls to run against Herman Talmadge!"

You said something like: "By God, I'll show you!" And you did. You took on Talmadge and what was left of the old Wool Hat Boys. Talmadge beat your socks off in the 1980 Democratic runoff for the Senate. Then he lost to a Republican named Mack Mattingly. That was about the biggest thing that happened in Georgia politics in the 1980s.

Nothing much changed. The Republican lasted one term. You stayed on as lieutenant governor. Tom Murphy, who helped Talmadge, kept the House speaker's office and tormented you every way he could think of. We replaced one unexciting governor with an even duller one. The state started going broke.

It looked for a while as if running against Talmadge was the worst career move you could have made. You became a political pariah. Most of the political establishment didn't even want to be seen with you.

In 1984, you chaired the state campaign for liberal Democratic presidential candidate Walter Mondale; the state went overwhelmingly for Ronald Reagan. Too bad — you might have been Mondale's secretary of education if he had won. He never had a chance. Everybody except you seemed to know that.

Eighteen months ago, the Joe Frank Harris crowd openly snubbed you as you began your campaign to bring a lottery to Georgia. Of course, Tom Murphy and his boys in the House and all their lobbyist buddies tried their best to keep you from winning the Democratic nomination in last summer's primary.

Now here it is 1991. You're about to become governor. Some of the boys and I thought we would drop you a note to say congratulations and to remind you how you said you'd change things if you ever got a chance. Now you've got it. You'll be governor of the biggest state east of the Mississippi, a governor with more legal power than almost any other state chief executive.

So what are you going to do first? Give us a lottery? You promised us that in every speech you made and every TV minute you bought. Will that change things? Or will it just create another monstrous bureaucracy loaded with fat patronage jobs for gubernatorial pals and plum accounts for bankers who played ball with your campaign?

Before we start playing Wheel of Fortune, Georgia-style, some of us wonder what you plan to do about the state's being busted. Depending on which of those Merit System bean counters you talk to, the state is either $333 million or $550 million in the red.

You have promised to address an estimated $501 million worth of public-school improvements. How are you going to pay for them? With borrowed money?

Your predecessor, Joe Frank Harris, thought that was one solution to our needs. When he took office in 1983, the state owed $1.385 billion in bonded debts. When he exits the Capitol this month, the state will owe $2.058 billion in bonded debt. That's a 50 percent increase in eight years.

We still have a third-rate education system. Transportation remains a nightmare. The state bureaucracy is bloated. We're still broke. As you always said, you can't borrow your way out of debt. If Georgia were a person instead of a state, it would be standing on 14th Street, holding up a sign that reads: "WILL DO ANYTHING FOR MONEY."

Ah, Zell, we're sounding like nags. We don't mean to. But you have succeeded. You're on top. You can do what you want now.

You could cure many of the state's ills simply and quickly. Go for another increase in taxes. Change the state's income-tax brackets to produce another billion or so dollars. You have said you intend to serve only one term. Another increase in taxes will make certain you keep that promise.

Or you could do nothing. You could just hunker down and hope the economy perks up and produces more revenue. We'll just keep rocking along as we have for the past century, benighted and bedraggled. Glad to have Mississippi and Alabama in our region; they keep folks from saying we're the worst.

Or you could try to reinvent state government. Assail the entrenched bureaucracy. Start from scratch. You could stop trying to improve schools by hurling more dollars at them. You could find out what's really wrong. You've said it yourself: You have taught in college and universities in this state. You are an accomplished author, historian, and lecturer. Still, you aren't qualified to teach high school. Because you never received a degree in education.

The education bureaucracy is so big and powerful that neither the Legislature nor the governor dares buck it by suggesting that the problem with education may be lousy teachers and the way they are taught to teach.

Public schools are just one part of the state's broken-down machinery that needs fixing. Look at some other cracks that need plugging up:

• Government Corruption: The matter of campaign contributions has been described by the state Supreme Court as bordering on bribery or extortion. Yet it seems impossible to enact legislation aimed at this problem. Shouldn't candidates for public office swear they will take no part in governmental actions regarding contributors of large sums to their campaigns? Shouldn't we have a law that requires that?

• Public Employment: The National Conference of State Legislatures makes an annual report on the number of state and local employees on government payrolls. The latest report shows that, on a per-capita basis, only six states in the nation (and no other state in the Southeast) have more public employees per capita than Georgia. It has been estimated that if Georgia's public employment—state and local government positions—were in line with other states', our taxpayers would save the equivalent of a one-cent sales tax.

The total number of state employees increased from 54,189 in 1983 to 66,325 in 1989. The number of patronage posts, those jobs going to people with political "pull" and those who did not have to take the competitive Merit System test, grew from 6,227 in 1983 to 12,787 at last count. That represents a breathtaking 105 percent increase in the number of patronage jobs handed out by the governor and Legislature.

• Transportation: The state's Transportation Department is a giant organization dedicated almost exclusively to laying asphalt.

Zell, will you have time to get serious about transportation and advocate a rail system that would connect Georgia's principal cities? Are you willing to say MARTA ought to be restructured, not as an Atlanta fiefdom, but as a statewide transit authority?

• Health Care: Doctors are abandoning our rural areas. What's going to be done about that?

AIDS and drug abuse have reached epidemic proportions. On the other hand, AIDS has captured so many headlines that researchers tell me public funds for more research on cancer, heart disease, and other killer illnesses are becoming increasingly hard to find. All the money is going to AIDS research.

Don't we need someone to stand up and say we must establish priorities for health care in this state?

• The Environment: The Congress has approved clean-air legislation that will force certain kinds of industries to abandon urban areas of our state. We may see harsh restrictions placed on the use of everything from power mowers to cigarette lighters in the metro Atlanta area.

Even more important, we are in a water crisis. Alabama and Florida have initiated litigation that will, in effect, put a cap on Atlanta's water supply. Gov. Harris tried unsuccessfully to negotiate the water problem with our sister states. Suppressing Atlanta's water supply is potentially the most profound long-term obstacle to Atlanta's growth facing the new administration.

• Prisons: If present trends continue, Georgia will have 60,000 men and women in prison by the year 2000. We can't afford to keep building prisons and locking people up ad infinitum. Still, lawlessness continues to rise. Atlanta ranks near the top nationally in violent crime. The state's crime rate is up dramatically.

This knotty problem requires imaginative solutions. Boot camps for first-time convicts may be good television, but it fails to answer the question: Are we ready to spend the millions, maybe billions, necessary to lock up the growing criminal population of Georgia?

• Higher Education: Faculty salaries at Georgia's four-year colleges have slipped from second to sixth in the region in just six years, and they are still going down. Significant economic growth, the kind of growth we want, will not come to our state if we do not maintain better than just-adequate research institutions.

These are only a few of our problems. Their solutions begin with the state budget process. Georgia's budget may look like a ledger of numbers. In reality, it is a statement of public policy and government agendas. It is also incomprehensible, even to many of those lawmakers who help formulate it.

The so-called supplemental budget should be abolished. Republicans and a handful of Democratic fiscal experts have advocated that move for years. The supplemental budget (the spending agenda for the current year) is a haven for pork-barrel projects and serves as a hiding place for other excessive expenditures. The General Assembly spends twice as much time annually on the supplemental budget as it does in preparing the budget for the coming year.

Your Republican opponent, Johnny Isakson, by the way, came up with a detailed plan for overhauling the budget. He deserves applause for that. You ought to consider enlisting his help in revamping the budget process.

To your credit, Zell, you stopped talking about the lottery just long enough to promise to create a budget review office. We just wanted to remind you.

One other thing, Zell: The state competes too often with private business. It should get out of running resorts and excursion railroads and should consider privatizing the operations of prisons and certain hospitals.

Georgia should also abandon the self-insurance business. The cost of the State Employees and Teachers Health Insurance program is rising by more than 20 percent per year. If dramatic action is not taken to control the cost of insuring these employees, that insurance program will consume all the state budget by 1996.

Zell, you have our sympathy. We understand there is just so much a governor can do, especially one strapped with a mediocre, self-centered, one-party Legislature and a cadre of special-interest lobbyists as entrenched in the General Assembly as blocks of rock.

We know you avoided getting tangled up with that crowd. We noticed you didn't take but a couple of million dollars from them for your campaign. Maybe you flew in their airplanes a few times.

Still, we know you meant what you said back there in the 1970s at The Little Mug: It's time for change.

You couldn't do much about it then, but you can now. We count on great creative changes to come in the 1990s, changes that will improve our quality of life and make government more responsive and less expensive.

We *can* count on that, right, Zell?

Happy New Year, Gov. Miller, from your old buddies at The Little Mug.

But What About the Other Great Killer?

Syndicated column—January 6, 1991

As a father whose son's life was snuffed out by a drunken driver, I applaud Gov.-elect Zell Miller's proposals to crack down on DUI.

Miller deserves praise from every quarter for his tough stand. Only the American Civil Liberties Union has suggested his ideas for punishing and humiliating drunk motorists are "goofy."

The General Assembly is all but certain to pass Miller's anti-DUI package. The courts, later on, may discover that a few rights have been trampled. But, hey, Miller and the politicians have made their point.

Drinking and driving ought to drop dramatically as a result.

Now let's see what our incoming governor and the General Assembly intend to do about another great killer of young people in Georgia—firearms.

Did you know that guns kill almost as many people in Georgia as drunk drivers? In the black community, firearms kill more people than liquored-up motorists. Murder, mostly by shooting, is the leading cause of death among young blacks.

In 1989, the State Patrol reported 553 persons were killed in motor-vehicle accidents in Georgia in which at least one driver was legally drunk. That same year, according to the FBI, firearms took 491 lives in Georgia. That does not count accidental shootings.

In 1988, a total of 498 persons died in accidents that involved a drunk driver; 448 died of gunshots.

While the number of deaths at the hands of drunken drivers has stabilized over the past five years, fatalities from shooting have steadily risen, from 398 in 1986 to 491 in 1989. The numbers from 1990 are not yet in.

Thanks to Gov. Joe Frank Harris and Mothers Against Drunk Drivers, Georgia already has adopted fairly rigid DUI laws.

MADD, led mostly by white middle-class parents whose children have been killed or maimed by drunken driving, is among the most effective lobbies in the state.

Black moms whose sons have been shot to death have little clout in the Statehouse.

But the National Rifle Association does. And Georgia has on its books the weakest firearms-control laws in the nation. A recent study of crime in Boston revealed, amazingly, that most of the weapons used were purchased in our state, nearly a thousand miles away.

Don't expect to hear any clarion call for controlling gun sales from the Miller administration or leaders of the Legislature. The National Rifle Association, the "sportsmen's" outfit that defends the sale to the public of assault rifles, regards Miller and House Speaker Tom Murphy, D-Bremen, as model public officials.

The NRA has rated both as "excellent" on lawmaking related to selling guns.

Gov.-elect Miller may tell you that DUI and gun control are unrelated. He may say owning a firearm is sewn into the cultural fabric of the South. So are making and drinking booze and driving fast cars.

The liquor industry poured tens of thousands of dollars into Miller's campaign for governor. That same industry wisely has endorsed tougher laws on drunken driving.

The National Rifle Association also gave heavily to Miller's campaign for governor. It distributed thousands of "Sportsmen for Miller" bumper stickers.

Unlike the whiskey companies, the NRA has no interest in mounting a public-relations campaign aimed at controlling the distribution of its products.

So while Miller's campaign against DUI may reduce auto-accident fatalities, you will see the gunshot homicide rate continue to rise.

Don't expect to hear a peep out of Miller about slowing down the sale of firearms in the state.

His DUI proposals are sound, but they took little courage to offer. Public opinion was on his side. A bit more bristle might be required to take up restricting the purchase of guns.

To this day, Georgia has one of the most liberal sets of firearms laws in the nation. And Miller did not succeed in getting most of his anti-DUI package enacted until 1997.

Will Justice Department Edict Split State's Democratic Coalition?

Syndicated column—July 14, 1991

A storm is building over the body politic of Georgia.

You have to go back to the early 1960s at the beginning of the civil rights era to find the state so close to the brink of major political change.

A recent note to the Mississippi Senate Elections Committee from the Justice Department is a harbinger of things to come in Georgia. The Justice Department, considering Mississippi's legislative redistricting plan, observed in its letter to the Mississippi committee:

"We note at the outset that the proposed districting plan for both the House and the Senate appear to have no retrogressive effect. ... Both plans maintain or expand the number of districts in which minority voters usually will be able to elect legislators of their choice."

After those words of praise, the Justice Department flatly rejected Mississippi's redistricting plan and ordered it to create even more minority-controlled legislative districts. The Justice Department strongly implied Mississippi ought to construct a legislature that reflects the black/white ratio of its population.

What does that portend for Georgia?

—Attorney General Mike Bowers believes the Justice Department will settle only for a Georgia redistricting plan that mirrors our population. If he is right, that means the Legislature must adopt a plan with about 45 minority districts in the 180-member House, and 15 minority seats in the 56-member Senate. The House currently has 27 black members; the Senate has eight.

—A possible end to majority rule in the state. Lawsuits attacking Georgia's majority-vote elections and method of choosing judges are pending in Brunswick, Atlanta, and Washington. The Justice Department, along with Rep. Tyrone Brooks, D-Atlanta, are parties to those lawsuits. Settlement of those cases is tied inextricably to legislative redistricting.

The Justice Department has insisted the state embrace a plurality method of elections. North Carolina, facing the same kind of pressure from Washington, already has adopted plurality elections.

"The Justice Department's premise is that racial bloc voting exists, and, therefore, we should maximize black voting strength by creating more black voting districts and eliminate the majority-vote requirement," says Bowers. "The ramifications of that are tremendous. It could mean an end to Democratic coalition politics."

It also could mean that racially polarized voting will be magnified.

If that happens, some observers believe political integration will come to a screeching halt. Georgia and the rest of the South could return to a "separate but equal" system of governance.

Consider the problem the Legislature will have in creating so many black-controlled districts. It must necessarily squeeze every black precinct into those districts.

That will leave lily-white districts, far outnumbering the blacks, in every corner of the state. The Bush administration's insistence on maximizing black voting power could have the reverse effect.

Consensus legislators—those who represent the views of both black and white constituents from their districts—could all but disappear.

Georgia is currently a one-party state, controlled by Democrats who derive their power from a black-white political alliance.

The reapportionment plan that finally emerges for Georgia could shatter that combination. It also could end the domination of the Democratic Party.

A conservative white Republican Party could replace the Democrats at the top. While the number of black lawmakers might increase, they could emerge with even less influence than they now wield.

The General Assembly will try in a special session in August to meet the Justice Department's demands for redistricting. Racial tensions are bound to develop. Gov. Zell Miller has charged that same special session with cutting up to $400 million from the state budget. Much of that reduction will come from programs that help the poor and minorities. That may intensify the bitterness that will grow out of the debate over redistricting.

The Dog Days of 1991 may not be remembered as the best of times in Georgia politics. "The next five years, starting in August, could be Reconstruction revisited," says one politician who doesn't want his name used.

The reapportionment fuss went on throughout much of the decade. The U.S. Supreme Court finally ruled in 1997 that Georgia's latest congressional reapportionment map, drawn by the courts, was OK.

The End of an Era
Coming Up

Syndicated column—January 26, 1992

The Old Guard of the Gold Dome is about to be dismissed. When the 1992 General Assembly adjourns in the spring, Georgia will be headed in a brand-new political direction. New faces and new policies will soon dominate the Capitol and the congressional delegation.

—The state will have at least three predominantly black congressional districts.

—It will have more than a dozen new black senatorial districts and at least 40 black state House districts.

—It will be on the verge of abandoning runoff primaries in favor of a plurality system of voting.

—Conservative whites, mostly suburban Republicans, will be preparing for the celebration of the century. They are about to take charge of state government and the Georgia congressional delegation.

And they can thank Rep. Tyrone Brooks, D-Atlanta, Rep. Cynthia McKinney, D-Atlanta, the American Civil Liberties Union, the Justice Department, and Gov. Zell Miller for helping them reach that mountaintop.

Here's why. Reps. Brooks and McKinney, with the expert help of ACLU lawyers, are pushing a "max black" redistricting plan that ensures the creation of new black legislative and congressional districts. The Justice Department has concurred with their proposals.

So the Legislature has set to work carving out curiously shaped districts that will engulf black voting power in every corner of the state. Those black districts are all but certain to elect minority lawmakers.

When the dust settles, African Americans will have more representation in the House, Senate, and the congressional delegation than ever.

Still, blacks will be.in the minority. Once-racially mixed legislative districts will be gone. Black voters will be lumped into nearly all-black districts. The next Legislature will be dominated by members from lily-white districts who will have little political incentive to consider minority issues.

Meantime, Gov. Miller says the reapportionment issue and anti-discriminatory litigation cannot be settled unless the state abandons its majority-wins voting system. John R. Dunne, the Justice Department's civil-rights chief, has told state officials he believes plurality elections will diminish racially polarized voting.

Miller has set the stage for the Super Bowl political battle of his administration. Attorney General Mike Bowers, once Miller's close ally, is adamantly opposed to scrapping majority elections.

House Speaker Tom Murphy, D-Bremen, has said repeatedly he opposes plurality elections. He doubts voters would approve a constitutional amendment overturning rule by majority elections.

Still, the betting here is that the pro-plurality crowd will prevail.

Add to this recipe for wholesale change the retirements of the state's most influential Democratic congressmen: 9th District Rep. Ed Jenkins, D-Jasper, 10th District Rep. Doug Barnard, D-Augusta, and 1st District Rep. Lindsay Thomas, D-Statesboro.

At least three other U.S. representatives—3rd District Rep. Richard Ray, D-Perry, 2nd District Rep. Charles Hatcher, D-Newton, and 4th District Rep. Ben Jones, D-Covington—are in jeopardy.

Sen. Wyche Fowler, D-Atlanta, is considered among incumbents vulnerable to defeat in the Senate.

Nearly half of Georgia's next congressional delegation will be freshmen. At least four—and perhaps five—will be Republicans.

If you doubt a new day is coming in Georgia politics, just wait. The handwriting is on the walls of the Legislature: The Democratic coalition that has controlled Georgia politics since the end of Reconstruction is about to collapse. What follows may be much different—but not necessarily much better.

If Duke Is Banned, It Could
Be You and Me Next

Syndicated column—February 2, 1992

Is David Duke a genuine Republican presidential candidate?

The American Civil Liberties Union makes a compelling argument that he is. And the ACLU is asking the 11th U.S. Circuit Court of Appeals to order Secretary of State Max Cleland to place Duke's name on Georgia's March 3 presidential primary ballot.

Never mind that Duke is a past imperial wizard (or was it a grand cyclops?) of the Ku Klux Klan and a one-time Nazi sympathizer.

Former KKK leader J. B. Stoner had a much worse record as a racist and terrorist. Yet the Georgia Democratic Party repeatedly placed him on its ballots. He invariably lost elections by lopsided margins to mainstream Democrats, including Zell Miller in a contest for lieutenant governor in 1978.

Stoner served a worthwhile purpose in his campaigns of hate. He was a gauge of malice and anti-Semitism. Over the years, his popularity at the polls declined until he finally slid into oblivion.

Back to the present: State GOP Chairman Alec Poitevint has protested that Duke is not a bona fide Republican and, therefore, should not appear on the Republican presidential ballot. The Republicans simply don't want Duke as a member of their party, Poitevint says.

If Duke wants to run in the presidential primary, let him run as an independent candidate and collect enough names on a petition to get on the ballot, says the Republican hierarchy. The petition route to getting on the ballot is costly and complicated and nearly impossible to achieve in Georgia.

In a lower-court decision last week, U.S. District Judge Richard Freeman agreed with his fellow Republicans' objections to Duke. As of now, Duke is off the Georgia ballot.

Despite his history of bigotry, Duke appears to qualify more as a Republican candidate than, say, conservative columnist Pat Buchanan, who has never stood for public office but whose name will be printed on the GOP presidential ballot.

In contrast to Buchanan, Duke meets every criterion of a genuine candidate with solid partisan credentials.

Duke is currently a Louisiana state representative, elected under the Republican banner.

Duke ran as a Republican for the U.S. Senate in 1990 and received 44 percent of the vote.

Duke ran as a Republican for governor of Louisiana in 1991 and won 39 percent of the vote.

Duke has qualified to appear on ballots in Republican presidential primaries in Massachusetts, Michigan, Mississippi, Louisiana, Tennessee, and Texas.

If David Duke quacks like a Republican candidate, looks like a Republican candidate, and wins office as a Republican candidate, then he must be a Republican candidate.

Nope, says GOP Chief Poitevint, he is not one of us. He is not a Republican. We don't want him in our club. Therefore, he can't be on the Republican ballot.

Southern Democrats used precisely the same argument against blacks in maintaining white primaries until 1944. They said they were free to exclude anyone they wished — and that meant the black voter — from participating in the Democratic Party.

In abolishing the white primaries, the Supreme Court held that political parties are not private clubs but public, state-sponsored entities. It held further that a person may not be excluded from the Democratic or Republican parties because of race, religion — or beliefs.

In Georgia, a citizen becomes a Democrat or a Republican simply by declaring his party preference.

If David Duke says in Georgia that he is a Republican, then he is one.

I am not a defender of Duke's philosophy. I have covered his hatemongering for over a dozen years in the light of fiery crosses in Alabama to Klan gatherings in Forsyth County, Georgia. I detest what he stands for.

But there is something disturbing about excluding him from the presidential race.

On TV last week, a young woman, waving a sign protesting a Duke press conference, told a reporter: "We don't want David Duke to speak because he is a fascist."

That is roughly why the Republicans don't want him in their midst. Still, if Duke can be barred in 1992 because he is an ex-Kluxer, could the Republicans or Democrats keep you and me from participating in a future election because we favor family planning, or profess belief in the Rosicrucians or are card-carrying Kiwanians?

That may sound absurd, but consider this: Not so long ago in Georgia, belonging to the Ku Klux Klan was politically correct if you were a white non-Catholic, non-Jewish male. In those days, David Duke would have been welcomed as a right-thinking centrist candidate.

Time to Strike Confederate Symbol and Move On

Syndicated column—May 30, 1992

The 1956 Georgia flag—the one that encompasses the Confederate battle banner—has a deep and special meaning to about one-third of the state's population.

To those African-American Georgians, it is a symbol of white supremacy, of defiance of court orders, of racial hatred.

To most Georgians, it is a vaguely sentimental reminder that our beloved South waged a war 130 years ago that never should have been fought, a war whose aftermath still stunts our growth and progress.

It is time the Confederate battle flag was struck.

Gov. Zell Miller announced Thursday morning to a group of business, religious, and civic leaders that he intended to sponsor a bill to change the state flag. He received a spontaneous standing ovation at that private gathering in the governor's office.

Sure, there were a few objections and regrets. House Speaker Tom Murphy says he intends to vote against the change. Some Murphy supporters say Miller's announcement was poorly timed because it will hurt the re-election chances of Democrats in conservative rural Georgia.

Maybe. Yet the king of the conservatives, U.S. House Republican Whip Newt Gingrich, supports Miller's idea. Months before Gov. Miller announced his proposal, Mike Bowers, the tough-minded law-and-order attorney general, publicly advocated changing the flag. He said it was an "insult" to black citizens. No one has ever accused Bowers of being soft on Southern tradition.

Immediately after Miller's press conference on the flag change, a Republican senatorial candidate, Charles Tanksley, held a press conference in the Capitol rotunda. He was there to denounce his GOP primary opposition for failing to campaign fairly. Someone asked Tanksley how he felt about "dropping the flag of our fathers."

Tanksley, a native son of Georgia, said the Confederate symbol should have been deleted from our official flag long ago. Then he went on to other subjects more dear to his heart, like how he might defeat Paul Coverdell and Wyche Fowler Jr. for the Senate.

As for Miller's role in the flag affair, he has said repeatedly: "There are more important issues than the flag." And there are. Miller's cheerleaders say the governor showed "uncommon courage" in planning a legislative farewell to the flag. A word of praise for Miller indeed may be in order.

Miller hopes to play a role in national Democratic politics in the future. He will receive national recognition for moving to dump a symbol of racial divisiveness. Besides, a Confederate flag is not much of a backdrop for an ambitious politician. The late Sen. Richard Russell found that out the hard way.

Miller's recent predecessors—Jimmy Carter, George Busbee, or Joe Frank Harris—could have disposed of the flag issue long ago without much political damage. In the 1970s, Rep. Janet Meritt, D-Americus, repeatedly offered resolutions in the House to change the flag.

Business leaders, especially those involved in multinational commerce, have long winced at the sight of the Confederate flag as an official symbol of their home state.

You won't find ranking executives of airlines, utility companies, or soft-drink makers longing to see the Confederate flag still flying over Georgia. Promoters of industry and trade have quietly tried to drop the Georgia flag from official ceremonies that might be observed by executives interested in locating in Georgia.

Even Civil War buffs and those who long for restoring "The Lost Cause" have difficulty explaining the 1956 flag. "It is a living memorial to the Confederacy," their brochures say.

That is not quite accurate. The flag was devised as a symbol of rebellion to court-ordered desegregation in the 1950s and 1960s. The previous flag—the Stars and Bars—was the Confederate commemorative.

More recently, the Georgia flag was used as one excuse by black vandals to stage violence in downtown Atlanta.

Now Miller has moved to remove a symbol of segregation and a reason for riot. He also has tried to head off a media circus over changing the flag.

By the time the 1993 Legislature convenes, headlines about the flag will be mostly forgotten. The symbolic issue should be handled with dispatch. And Miller and the lawmakers can get on with substantive matters, like improving schools, consolidating counties, planning the lottery, and divvying up pork-barrel projects.

The Lottery and Other Sins

Georgia Trend—October 1992

Liquor store owners in Atlanta once worked hand in glove with some Baptist preachers in Cobb County to keep Cobb "dry." And they succeeded for decades. The suburban Baptists held the moral high ground that the vice of alcohol use should not be permitted—and certainly should not be sanctioned by the local government.

The package store operators were pragmatic business people. They reasoned if thirsty Cobb Countians couldn't buy booze legally in Cobb, they would have to cross the Chattahoochee to purchase it in Fulton. Liquor stores lined the Fulton banks of the 'Hooch. "Wanna make a run to the river?" was as standard a question in Marietta and Smyrna as, say, "Is it hot enough for you?"

The Baptists' zeal and the liquor men's money defeated referendum after referendum on letting Cobb go wet until well into the 1950s. Whether their coalition saved any souls from John Barleycorn is debatable. There's no question it cost Cobb millions of dollars in tax revenue.

We are seeing an updated version of that Baptists-and-booze debate. Only this time, the issue is gambling; the battle lines are more complex, and the arguments on both sides more compelling.

On Nov. 3, voters will have an opportunity to decide whether Georgia will run a state-sponsored lottery. Gov. Zell Miller promises the game will funnel additional millions for education into the state's coffers.

Opposition to the lottery is fierce. From some Protestant clergymen who oppose it on moral grounds. From legal gambling interests in Florida and Alabama who see Georgia's entry into the gaming field as keeping Georgia customers at home and siphoning profits. From illegal lottery operators who fear legalized games will lure away their regulars from the nickel, dime, and penny "bug" games.

And from elected school superintendents who have joined the preachers in the fight against Miller's "Georgians for Better Education" campaign. The governor has linked—some believe unwisely—the campaign for a constitutional amendment authorizing the lottery to a second amendment that would require all school chiefs to be appointed by elected local boards of education. The measure has the effect of destroying the political fiefdoms of elected school supers in nearly every corner of the state.

It also has the effect of creating an unholy union of preachers and political bosses, determined to defeat a common enemy but for different reasons, just like the keep-our-county-dry allies of three or four decades ago.

Opponents of the education lottery say it has been used in other states—Florida, for example—to reduce regular appropriations for schools. Therefore, education has not been enhanced by gambling dollars; it has been hurt.

Besides, the say-no-to-the-numbers crowd argues, a state lottery would induce poor people to waste their money on gaming in the nearly always vain hope of becoming wealthy.

Should Georgia state government, here in the buckle of the Bible Belt, operate gambling games? Should the state advertise and operate vice? the lottery opposition asks rhetorically. Let's look at those issues:

THE FLORIDA EXAMPLE: Gov. Lawton Chiles of Florida says that state's lottery has turned out to be "fraud." In February, *Florida Trend* magazine reported: "... Of the more than $3.2 billion in profits generated by the lottery, only about one-third of that amount appears to have truly enhanced education. The remainder has supplanted funds education was previously receiving from general revenue. In essence, the lottery has become a big shell game."

"That can't happen—and won't happen—in Georgia," Zell Miller promises. Why? Because the Georgia lottery law contains a guarantee that lottery funds cannot be used as a substitute for regular appropriations by the Legislature.

Says the Georgia Lottery for Education Act: "No surplus in the Lottery for Education Account shall be reduced to correct any nonlottery deficiencies in sums available for general appropriations, and no surplus in the Lottery for Education Account shall be included in any surplus calculated for setting aside nonlottery reserve or midyear adjustment reserve."

So that takes care of that opposition argument, right? Maybe not.

The 1987 statute creating the Florida lottery clearly states: "The net proceeds of lottery games [must] be used to support improvements in public education and that such proceeds not be used as a substitute for existing resources."

As the recession deepened and Florida's revenues slipped, that provision of the lottery law was ignored in the final budget decisions of the state's Legislature and governor.

PROTECTING THE POOR: There is stark proof in the lottery debate that the plantation mentality and elite paternalism are still alive and well in our state. The enlightened foes of the lottery have said repeatedly they are determined to save the poor from themselves. They may be barking up the wrong tree.

The notion that the lottery is a poor man's game may be baloney. Opponents of state lotteries oppose it on grounds that it encourages gambling by persons who should be buying baby formula and granola instead of numbers tickets.

A number of studies indicate the lottery is a middle-class pastime. In New Jersey, the R. H. Bruskin Associates research group found 33 percent of the players had income of $25,000 to $90,000 a year; 22 percent made at least $40,000 a year; and 82 percent made over $15,000. The researchers concluded that a majority of lottery players in New Jersey are married, middle-class Caucasians with an education level of high school or higher.

Studies in other areas, including the South, reached similar conclusions.

A footnote: Poor blacks for years have spent pennies and nickels on the illegal "bug" games played around the state. The games are based on security-market numbers published in the newspaper.

The "bug" is such big business in Atlanta that illegal lottery operators regularly hold "conventions" in the city to compare notes. The "bug" operators could organize opposition to the legal lottery in the black community. If that materializes, it could lose.

DO GEORGIANS REALLY WANT A LOTTERY? Sixty-eight percent of them do, according to a Georgia State University poll conducted in June 1992. Governor Zell Miller used the promise of a lottery as the centerpiece of his successful campaign for governor in 1990.

The governor's background paper on the lottery points out: "Thirty-nine states already have lotteries, including Florida, where substantial Georgia money goes every week. Georgians are playing the Florida lottery to the tune of at least $200 million a year since it began in 1988. Seven of the 10 biggest outlets for the Florida lottery are on the Florida-Georgia state line. Don Morris, who owns a store on U.S. 301, a hundred feet south of the Florida-Georgia line, estimates that three-fourths of his lottery customers are Georgians.

"In fact, Georgians have won a total of $25 million from the Florida games since 1989."

Making a convincing case against a legal lottery is difficult. Lotteries across the country have been successful because people enjoy playing them. In some places, the lottery fad has worn thin, and the number of players is down. Still, millions of dollars continue to roll in.

A picture of the mob moving in to take over the lottery games is fiction. There has never been a major fraud in a state lottery. Computerized lottery systems provide nearly foolproof security systems.

Won't the lottery open the door to legalized horse betting and even casinos down the road? Probably, although Georgia's present lottery law specifically prohibits pari-mutuel betting. A number of states have moved from lottery to horse tracks (and dog tracks, ugh!) and even full-service gambling houses. That is not likely to occur in Georgia for years. In the end, of course, there is not much disagreement that gambling is not a virtuous pursuit. But sin is relative.

"Which is the greater sin?" asks Miller's senior aide, Steve Wrigley. "To play the lottery? Or to sit idly by, knowing that one out of three children entering a Georgia kindergarten will drop out of school before graduation? Money from the lottery will help remedy that problem and improve education generally.

"Is that a sin?"

The Georgia lottery became one of the most successful state-sponsored gaming enterprises in the country. Gov. Zell Miller's lottery-financed HOPE scholarship program received national acclaim.

What Would Dr. King Think of His Dream Now?

Syndicated column — April 7, 1993

Suppose Dr. Martin Luther King Jr. had dodged James Earl Ray's bullet. Suppose Dr. King had lived. There would be no King holiday and no memorials to his death or his great moments in life. His "I Have a Dream" speech in Washington might have been forgotten.

Even if it weren't, would Dr. King, at age 64, today believe his dream had come true, that his nation in 1993 is a place where individual character has become more important than race? Probably not.

The papers were filled last weekend with stories marking the 25th anniversary of Dr. King's murder.

Most of the accounts dealt with theories that the CIA and FBI were on the side of Dr. King's killer(s). HBO even staged a mock trial of James Earl Ray, and the TV jury acquitted the gunman.

Not much was said about Dr. King's dream. That avalanche of commemorative prose undoubtedly will come on the 30th anniversary of his speech in August.

The 1993 reality of Dr. King's 1963 dream is this:

All legal barriers to full black participation in society are gone. Most of those hurdles had fallen before Dr. King's death.

Blacks hold Cabinet posts, and the nation's top military commander is a black Army general. More black Americans are in the Congress than ever. Three members of Georgia's House delegation are black, one a female.

More than two dozen black citizens are members of the state Legislature.

Rep. Tyrone Brooks of Atlanta was recently elected president of the Georgia Association of Black Elected Officials, which boasts more than 500 members and is growing larger each year. Brooks is a protégé of one of King's lieutenants, Hosea Williams.

Another King aide, Andrew Young, has been a congressman, a United Nations ambassador, an Atlanta mayor, and a runner-up for governor. He helped bring the Olympics to Georgia, whose segregation laws once would have prohibited extending an invitation to the multiracial Games. Young is counted among the nation's most distinguished citizens.

Atlanta Mayor Maynard Jackson is a leading political light in urban America. Many of the nation's foremost sports and entertainment figures are black. And there is no shortage of black multimillionaires. There are more black lawyers and doctors and bankers than ever.

Dr. King dreamed one day that hundreds of thousands of blacks would become wealthy, well-educated, and upwardly mobile. Part of that dream has materialized.

On the other hand —

Blacks continue to occupy the lowest rungs on the country's economic ladder. Georgia leads the nation and much of the world in infant mortality because of the high pregnancy rate among the state's black teenagers.

Most of Georgia's welfare recipients are black. More than three-fourths of Georgia's prison population is black, yet blacks comprise only 25 percent of the state's residents. Crime in the black community continues to soar.

The state's school systems are becoming resegregated, with blacks attending public schools while whites enroll in increasing numbers in private institutions. The black dropout rate is appalling.

The Voting Rights Act, which Dr. King saw as a healing and uniting force in the 1960s, has been used to resegregate congressional districts and the Legislature.

The past legislative session was the most racially polarized General Assembly in memory.

Affirmative action and set-aside programs have helped some blacks, but not many. And they have given rise to cries of "reverse discrimination" and increased resentment.

Old-timers, who observed the civil rights movement in the 1960s, say the South is more divided and less optimistic about race relations today than it was then.

They also lament that Dr. King's call for individual freedom has been lost in current campaigns for "group rights" and "cultural diversity." Nonviolent dissent—the life blood of the civil rights movement—has been drowned out by demands for political correctness.

Part of Dr. King's dream has been fulfilled, but the nightmare lingers.

When 'Gay' Is Angry, and 'Simple' Is Complex

Syndicated column—August 25, 1993

Future historians may have trouble deciphering what really occurred on this portion of the planet in the 1990s.

The reason: Double-speak—they call it political correctness now—is back in vogue. Ordinary English words have taken on double meanings. Simple statements of fact have turned into complex contradictions.

If Rip Van Winkle had suddenly awakened in Cobb County last weekend, he might have thought he was still asleep and in the midst of a linguistic nightmare.

A thousand people stood in the Marietta city square, waving signs proclaiming they were "gay." They didn't look especially gay, that is, merry or lighthearted. Most seemed angry and agitated and, some might say, a little whacked out. Rip might not have understood that in the last part of the 20th century "gay" is a politically correct adjective applied almost exclusively to male homosexuals.

If he had waited around an hour or so, he would have seen another crowd gather, this one hoisting banners in the name of "family values." In his mind's eye, Rip might have conjured up an old *Saturday Evening Post* cover with mom and pop and all the kids gathered round the Thanksgiving dinner table or unwrapping gifts on Christmas Day.

That is not the meaning of "family values," circa 1993. The phrase today is generally applied to groups who demand enactment of a law that would prohibit abortions, or believe prayer should be conducted in public schools, or can't understand why "gays" can't behave themselves and act un-gay.

The perversion of the language did not begin nor will it end with the homophobe-homophile doings in Cobb County. Double-speak is an ancient art form in politics and government, though it seems to be flourishing now more than ever.

For example, President Bill Clinton's recent "deficit reduction bill" was really a huge tax bill. Any deficit reduction mandated by the measure will occur, if ever, five or six years from now. The White

House press office insisted on calling it a "deficit reduction" plan, and the sheep in the media went along.

The "tax simplification" legislation of the early 1990s turned out to be the Accountants and Lawyers Welfare Act. The "simplification law" complicated the tax code so much that ordinary citizens were compelled to call on professional help in filing their returns.

"Law and order" have become code words for repression and discrimination. The words "enhanced user fees" were used in Georgia a couple of years ago to disguise a general tax increase wherein the levies were collected by sellers of car tags, drivers licenses, and hunting and fishing permits.

The latest and perhaps most egregious example of linguistic double-talk is again occurring in Washington. Before he went on vacation, President Clinton put on his conservative coat and tossed out for consideration by Congress his "anti-crime package." The public applauded. Pundits stroked their chins and noted, "The president is moving to the right."

There is a small defect in the legislation, say the president's critics. A major portion of the bill is not aimed at stamping out crime at all, but at eliminating the death penalty.

Florida Attorney General Robert Butterworth's office analyzed the bill and concluded that it creates nearly endless new avenues of appeal for convicted murderers sentenced to death.

And Georgia Attorney General Mike Bowers, an increasingly vocal antagonist of Clinton and many other Democrats, has written each member of the state's congressional delegation, asking him/her to vote against the president's "anti-crime bill" as it is now written.

"The changes do not reform the process. On the contrary, they would effectively repeal the death penalty," Bowers wrote. "Any student of this area of the law cannot deny the deleterious effects of this legislation."

Speaking of deceptive phrases, try this one in the Georgia Government Guide: "Michael J. Bowers, Democrat." Wouldn't it be more accurate to say, "Michael J. Bowers, not-quite-Democrat anymore"?

Shortly after this was written, Bowers made it official and switched to the Republican Party.

Schools Need More Than Bulletproofing

Syndicated column—September 22, 1993

So you thought money from the lottery would be used to transform our public schools into glistening computerized centers of knowledge?

Guess again. Improving the quality of Georgia's education is taking a back seat to making the schools bulletproof.

Gov. Zell Miller's principal annual address on education—traditionally a clarion call for more money for politically potent educators—sounded a dramatically different theme this year.

He says he'll ask the Legislature to change the formula for parceling out lottery funds for education. He wants to use $10 million in gambling proceeds to install metal detectors and police monitoring devices in schools. He vows to disarm the student population.

The presence of guns in the classrooms and shooting on the school grounds are replacing poorly prepared teachers and inadequate facilities as Georgia's most pressing education problems.

"I am afraid, if we don't take some measures, that in the not-too-distant future, we will know that school has started when we hear the sound of gunshots, and we will measure the pace of the school year by the deaths of students," Miller declared last weekend at the conclusion of the 1993 Governor's Conference on Education.

Three days before Miller announced his arms-reduction plan, Atlanta mayoral candidate Michael Lomax kicked off his campaign to move into City Hall with a similar tone: "It's time we provided shields for our children," he declared, promising to hire more policemen and take other measures to ensure Atlanta's streets and schools are cleansed of guns and gunmen.

Meanwhile, state School Supt. Werner Rogers' special Task Force on School Violence concluded that installing metal detectors at school entrances is one way to prevent shootists from disrupting classes.

All this public rhetoric about guns and rowdies is a result of the 1993-94 school year starting with a bang. In the first three weeks of

123

school, a half dozen serious incidents involving guns have been reported in metro Atlanta schools. At least two children have been shot.

In one instance, a student who forgot his pistol phoned his mother and asked her to bring it to him in school. She did, and was caught handing the piece to her son.

In several Georgia school districts, students are not allowed to carry book satchels or backpacks because they have been used to conceal weapons.

Even without the upsurge in violence, Georgia's public school system has been in steep decline for decades, as we continue to pour more money into it. During the last school year, Georgia taxpayers plunked down $4,860 per student in our public schools, ranking the state near the top in spending. Yet, we remain at or near the bottom in test scores that measure student achievement.

A national study suggests that as little as 33 cents of every school-tax dollar went for classroom instruction last year. The rest was spent for "administration."

The latest school crisis—guns in the classroom—means that an even smaller slice of the tax dollar will be spent for education and more for metal detectors and guards to prevent violence.

Gov. Miller, Supt. Rogers, and candidate Lomax ought to be commended for recognizing the problem. But they may be zeroing in on the wrong solution. The guns are only a symptom of what has happened to part of our school-age population. Certainly, keeping guns away from students is essential to maintaining safety. Still, a bad kid remains a bad kid, with or without a weapon.

Some of our braver political souls are finally going to have to face a harsher truth and more dramatic solution to the problem: If our public schools are to survive, they will have to be changed significantly.

We may have to establish one system of schools for those who seek an education and another for those who must be simply subdued.

A Time to Ask 'Why?' and 'What?'

Syndicated column — April 6, 1994

The space between the end of the legislative session and the beginning of the state election campaigns allows time for thought. That may not be a good thing for those holding elective office. Because the quiet period may produce questions about Georgia government for which there are no reasonable answers.

For instance:

• Why does the state of Georgia allow non-Georgian and, in some cases, non-American mining firms to extract billions of dollars worth of minerals from our soil without paying the state one cent in severance taxes?

• Why does the state insist on scheduling primary elections in the hottest part of summer, a time that ensures a sparse turnout of voters and serves as election insurance for incumbents?

Our election officials tell us mid-summer primaries are necessary to give the state time to print absentee ballots for "overseas Georgians" before the November general election. That's strange. Florida, with more than twice as many citizens, holds its primary in September, and there's still plenty of time to mail ballots to "overseas Floridians."

• Why do we support 159 counties, many of which have populations smaller than some residential subdivisions in urban Georgia? Who says we must waste money and resources on these tiny governments that exist only to collect state and federal subsidies?

• Why does Georgia continue to have the highest infant-death rate in the country and one of the highest in the world — although Georgians spend billions more each year on health care for indigent mothers and children?

• Why do we maintain a University System payroll bloated with tenured faculty members who do little work and cannot be fired? To be sure, many tenured professors are productive, but there are enough of the other kind to create genuine concern.

• Why is there so much debate and delay about striking a 1956 state flag that is clearly racist, especially when the alternative is returning to a historically significant banner that genuinely reflects our Southern heritage?

• Why do we tolerate a Legislature whose leaders refuse even to consider limiting their terms in office or giving citizens a direct voice in government?

• Why does state government refuse to budge on such wide-ranging problems as abating air pollution and making it easier to register to vote, until the federal government threatens to take away billions for highways?

• Why do we have elective labor and agriculture commissioners who do little more than administer federal programs, when we are not allowed to elect an auditor to watch over state government? Ironically, the Legislature, which requires the most scrutiny, presently hires and fires the state auditor.

• Why do we maintain a Public Service Commission, some of whose members are best known for their absenteeism? Why do we finance a PSC that lacks qualifications and staff to regulate the growing complexities of telecommunications and energy?

• Why does Georgia always rank highest in the "worst" categories: health care, violent crime, school dropouts, poor academic achievement, low-paying jobs, and just plain poverty?

• And why has state government abdicated so many of its responsibilities?

Our criminal justice system has broken down. Even the state's chief law enforcement officer, Attorney General Mike Bowers, says so. The public education system, at least the parts not supported by concerned local governments, is failing. The federal government has, by default, taken from state government the authority to protect our water, air, soil, and civil rights.

It is gradually taking full control of regulating communications, energy, transportation, and public assistance because the state can't or won't take on those responsibilities.

So before we get down to choosing state executives and legislators in the coming elections, perhaps we should ask: "Just what does state government, with its 110,000 employees and $10 billion budget, do for us anyway?"

A New Wave of Okies

AT&T Interchange — August 2, 1995

"In Atlanta, Georgia, there is now an African-American mayor, Bill Campbell, and an African-American majority on the city council. It seems a little strange to have white bureaucrats in Washington, D.C., deciding whether elected black Atlantans care about poor black Atlantans. By what right does a Washington bureaucrat have to stand in judgment of Mayor Campbell? What theory assumes that if you work in a federal office building you are morally superior to a local government official?"

So writes Speaker Newt Gingrich in his book, *To Renew America*. It sounds so simple. So right.

How can the pointy-headed liberals in Washington possibly know what is best for us in Alabama, Mississippi, Georgia, California, New York, Michigan, and so on?

The answer is, they can't. That is what's wrong with the national system of public assistance. The War on Poverty has been waged by out-of-touch generals who don't understand the enemy or the territory beyond the Beltway.

Gingrich and at least two presidential candidates, Sens. Robert Dole and Phil Gramm, have set out to clean up the welfare mess. President Clinton has weighed in with a reform plan of his own. All have said grassroots governments are best suited to administer dollars for the needy.

The House passed a bill in March that would provide block grants for state and local governments to administer welfare programs with minimal guidance from Washington.

Dole's proposal is similar to the House bill in that poor people no longer would be entitled to assistance, and the federal government would limit spending, regardless of economic need.

At a conference in Vermont, governors from both parties said they favor welfare plans that provide states with the most money and the fewest restrictions.

Therein lies the problem.

Most of us may agree that Washington has done a tragically inept job with public welfare. But are we ready to see billions of federal tax dollars turned over to state governments to do with as they please in helping (or not helping) the poor? How can Congress be so certain that the states and cities will perform better than the feds in administering aid for the indigent?

Advocates of letting the state and local governments hold the welfare purse contend those jurisdictions are more "efficient" and "cost-conscious" than Uncle Sam.

Really? Have the proponents of "Let the boys back home do it" considered the financial collapse of Orange County, Calif., the fiscal debacle of the government of West Virginia, the sensational corruption trials of Atlanta airport officials and dozens of other scandals in city halls and statehouses across the country?

Two years ago, Georgia Gov. Zell Miller's administration unveiled a state-based plan to provide health insurance for poor children. The scheme never got off the ground.

Giving the states a free hand to run public-assistance programs is akin to letting each do its own thing in protecting the environment. It just doesn't work.

The Federal Clean Water and Clean Air Acts grew out of the inability and, in some cases, downright refusal of states to abate pollution.

The states competed with each other to see which could offer the least-stringent pollution rules for industries. Such easy anti-pollution rules were, and still are, used to attract economic development.

Georgia is a prime example. The Chattahoochee River is becoming an open sewer because the state government and the city of Atlanta refuse to clean it up. The state Natural Resources Department, which imposed heavy fines on the city for failing to treat sewage, recently announced it would use some of the penalty money to build a park for Atlanta. Is that getting tough?

The U.S. Environmental Protection Agency, for reasons that are not entirely clear, has allowed Georgia to take the lead in enforcing anti-pollution rules. If you think that delegation of power has worked, take a look at and sniff the Chattahoochee at Atlanta. Unless the river is quickly cleansed, it may become a major embarrassment for the city and the state during the 1996 Olympics next summer.

State-run welfare programs also would become competitive under plans now before Congress, but in a different way. States are likely to compete with each other to make restrictions on welfare recipients so harsh that recipients would leave.

Welfare mothers would find themselves, more and more, seeking out states and cities for care, while local and state administrators would make that assistance as hard to come by as possible. Eventually, America may see the emergence of a new generation of impoverished migrants, much like the Depression-era Okies, roaming from state to state and city to city in search of help.

Speaker Gingrich has opened a national debate on several vital issues, welfare among them, for the first time in decades. We ought to thank him for that. But his ideas for reforming public assistance, like the bills to reduce environmental protection, need a good deal of fine-tuning.

The end of the welfare reform story has not been written. New laws have been passed that impose public-assistance deadlines on needy families. Some say those reforms are cruel. Others contend they will end the welfare cycle.

The Olympics' Biggest Challenge

Syndicated column—July 27, 1994

Twenty-two million Americans want to come to Georgia in 1996 for the Olympics. Those astonishing figures are included in two recent national marketing surveys, says Atlanta Olympics chief Billy Payne.

Of course, no such multitude is going to show up on our doorsteps just two summers from now. If they did, we couldn't handle them.

But hundreds of thousands of visitors from other states and nations will be here. Many will never have ventured away from home before. Some will know Atlanta and Georgia only as places described in *Gone with the Wind* or as the home of Coca-Cola.

When reporters and editors gathered last week for Payne's countdown luncheon on Olympics progress, they heard mostly good news. They learned little about how the Olympics managers plan to protect unwary visitors during the Games.

When a questioner with an attitude brought up Atlanta's lingering crime problem, Payne brushed it aside. Crime rates have traditionally fallen during the Olympics because of extraordinary security precautions, he said, and went on to the next topic.

Still, the question remains: How can Georgia authorities protect hundreds of thousands of tourists from predators in the Atlanta area, labeled by the FBI as the biggest pocket of violence in America?

A single significant incident in the summer of 1996 could destroy all the planning and work that have gone into making Georgia into an international showcase for the Centennial Games.

Who recalls the achievements of the 1972 Olympic athletes in Munich? Almost no one. For those Games were overshadowed by an invasion of terrorists that left 11 Israeli Olympians dead. Mention the Munich Games today, and the massacre is all that is remembered. Just a couple of weeks ago, Atlanta received a shocking reminder that it is not immune to out-of-the-blue violence against visitors. A Mexican Army doctor, touring the U.S. with his family, was shot to death during a robbery attempt in a motel parking lot in DeKalb County.

The Atlanta Chamber of Commerce understandably played down the tragedy as an isolated incident. Said a spokesman for the Chamber:

"There is not a pattern of crimes here where tourists are targeted. If that were the case, most of the crimes would occur near the airport."

A lawsuit pending before the Georgia Supreme Court suggests a pattern of crime against out-of-towners indeed has developed. In that case, Matt vs. Days Inns of America, the Court of Appeals has held that crime is rampant in the airport area. It ruled that Days Inn was negligent in allowing one of its patrons, Richard Matt, to be shot during a parking-lot holdup at the airport Days Inn last year.

Matt was wounded shortly after he and his new bride arrived at the motel. They were to leave the following morning on their honeymoon.

In the majority opinion for the Court of Appeals, Chief Judge A. W. Birdsong Jr. noted:

"The Matts ... introduced evidence that there were 82 crimes committed at the hotel in the three years preceding the attack on Richard Matt. ... In addition, the Matts introduced evidence showing that there are three other airport hotels within a one-quarter mile radius of the Days Inn, and that at one hotel there were 184 parking lot crimes, including five armed robberies, one strong-arm robbery, two rapes, ten assaults, and one kidnapping; another of the hotels had 257 parking lot crimes, including five armed robberies, one strong-arm robbery, one rape, and 26 assaults; and at the other hotel, three parking lot crimes, including two assaults and one kidnapping."

Days Inn has appealed the case to the Georgia Supreme Court. Business leaders are fearful the Matt case will establish a change in public policy whereby private enterprises will be required to accept an increasing amount of responsibility for the safety of their patrons.

More importantly, the Matt case and the more recent murder of Mexican Army Major Cesar Garcia point up the make-or-break challenge of the 1996 Olympics: to keep from harm's way the throngs of guests who will come here.

A bombing at Centennial Olympic Park, which killed one person, threatened to overshadow the 1996 Atlanta Games.

131

Newt Has Great Ideas, But ...

Syndicated column—March 12, 1995

House Speaker Newt Gingrich is perhaps the most eloquent and persuasive national figure Georgia has produced in decades.

In time, if he survives the unrelenting scrutiny of the big news media, Gingrich could have a more profound impact on the American destiny than, say, Georgia Sens. Richard Russell and Walter George or even Jimmy Carter and Dean Rusk.

Since I first covered Gingrich in the early 1970s, he has grown in stature from an unsure and sometimes awkward college lecturer to a confident and seamless orator. He has honed to a fine edge the talent of making the most radical assertions sound reasonable.

At a breakfast meeting last week, even yellow-dog Democrats found themselves nodding in agreement as Speaker Gingrich ticked off the sins of the federal government, ranging from formulating needless and arcane regulations to engaging in wasteful and corrupt work habits.

He heaped praise on Gov. Zell Miller, the chief of Georgia Democrats, who has received the lion's share of credit for installing Gingrich's main punching bag, Bill Clinton, in the White House.

Indeed, Gov. Miller seems on his way to becoming the speaker's most trusted buddy among Democrats, most of whom Gingrich detests.

Miller is the only Democratic governor to endorse Gingrich's reform of the school-lunch program.

The depth of Miller's dedication to the Gingrich line is uncertain. When an ABC-TV reporter asked the Georgia governor for an interview on his Newtonian Epiphany, Miller allowed as how he was "no longer granting national interviews." When he was seated next to a well-known journalist at an awards ceremony last week, the governor asked to be moved. He apparently did not want to be forced to make small talk about his new political pal, Speaker Newt.

Much of what Gingrich prescribes and Miller endorses makes sense. We need to reduce regulations and litigation. A meaningful federal tax cut is overdue. Our welfare system, which has created a vast class of parasitic bums, cries for an overhaul.

Yet, one theme in Gingrich's symphony of change is plain scary. Gingrich would assign massive federal programs—environmental protection, Medicaid, child welfare, etc.—back to the states to manage.

Consider what that would mean in the context of the Georgia Legislature. The federal government would ship billions of dollars back to Georgia to be administered by a General Assembly that just last week:

—Stripped the state budget of $5 million for law enforcement and education programs so it could buy Little League uniforms, fire trucks, and playground equipment to satisfy a handful of good old boys.

—Redirected $40 million for improvement of the port of Savannah to pork-barrel boondoggles. The governor had proposed the port renovation so Savannah might successfully compete against Charleston for a Home Depot distribution center that would create hundreds of jobs. The Legislature said no; it had bike paths to build, country roads to widen, and cheerleaders' uniforms to buy.

—Spent an entire day in the Senate debating whether to include religious references in teaching American history, but refused to enact a law that mandates publishing official documents in our mother tongue, which happens to be English.

—Saw Gingrich's Georgia counterpart, House Speaker Tom Murphy, show up in the back of the Senate chamber to deride the senators for considering a state tax reduction. "I wish I had a camera," Murphy told bystanders in the Senate. "I'd like to take a picture of these clowns. Did you ever see such clowns?"

This is the same Legislature and state government that have allowed the Chattahoochee River south of Atlanta to become a stream of untreated sewage. And it is the same Legislature that approved paying a third-rate, privately owned football team more than $4 million a year to play in a state stadium.

Get serious, Newt. If you believe Washington has made a mess of crime prevention, public assistance, and the environment, just wait until the boys under the Gold Dome in Atlanta get a crack at those programs and the dollars that go with them.

State government may not help the poor, stamp out crime, or clean up the air and water. But you can bet that, if you send billions in block grants to the state, there won't be a cow path left unpaved or a brother-in-law unhired.

The Dream that Went Awry

Syndicated column—April 5, 1995

There is an article of faith that has sustained political do-gooders for generations: Once the GOP gains a solid foothold in Georgia, and we have a genuine two-party democracy, we will have a more responsive and accountable state government.

In the November election, the dream came true. The Republicans picked up enough ground in the General Assembly to stop or start any movement they wished. They elected five of their own to the executive branch of state government. The most influential Republican in the nation—make that the world—emerged from east Cobb County: Newt Gingrich, the self-proclaimed foe of the corrupt status quo and the role model for every bushy-tailed new Republican in the Statehouse.

But, alas, the above-mentioned article of faith was shattered. A hundred Republicans in the Georgia House, the Senate, the congressional delegation, and constitutional offices did not produce better performance. Democrats did not become increasingly prudent. Republicans were not more watchful. Citizens did not benefit more.

In truth, state government in general, and the Legislature in particular, suffered a dumbing-down after the demise of one-party control. We can hope the stupor will pass during the next year or two.

One need review only a few actions of the past Legislature to realize that special interests, anarchy, and sometimes downright stupidity still prevailed in the wake of the Republican revolution. Consider:

— While no one was paying much attention, the Legislature set aside $16 million for legal fees as it enacted a bill to compensate federal retirees for being illegally taxed in the mid-1980s. About 100,000 pensioners may finally get cash reimbursement from the state.

Why the Legislature felt compelled to dole out $16 million to either one or two or three lawyers representing the retirees is unclear. The state's chief legal counsel, Attorney General Michael Bowers, advised the governor's office and the General Assembly to let the pensioners and their attorneys hash out among themselves the details of paying the legal fees.

After all, that is the usual procedure in most litigation. Not this time. No siree, the lawyer-dominated Legislature was going to see to it that their brothers at the Bar got their just desserts, all $16 million of them. To no one's surprise, such a grand sum inspired a stack of lawsuits, including one that would set aside the entire settlement for the retirees.

The pensioners may not receive a cent of what they are owed until the lawyers settle up.

The Republican watchdogs must have been asleep under the porch when the Democrats wheeled this treasure chest through the House and Senate.

—The GOP was obviously wide awake when the House and the Senate enacted a $242 million (some argue it was actually $292 million) tax break for property owners. A couple of Republicans even took credit for shepherding the bill to approval.

When the dust settled, it turned out that the tax-relief bill simply let property owners pay Uncle Sam what they had previously paid local governments in taxes. The bill was so huge that it soaked up all the money for highway improvements, state employee raises, and other functions for years to come.

Only eight legislators—six Democrats and two Republicans—saw the quickie tax bill in its final form. A carefully considered set of recommendations on badly needed revisions of the state tax code was brushed aside in the rush to pass, sight unseen, the "tax-relief" bill.

—The Republican sentinels apparently rolled over and went back to sleep when a $6 million item for "economic development" sailed through the Assembly. From that vague line in the budget comes a series of "forgivable" loans of your tax money to such needy worthies as Siemens, the mammoth German electronics firm, and McDonnell Douglas, the aerospace giant.

Is this the kind of diligence we can expect from the newly empowered minority party in our Legislature? If it is, we might have been better off in the bad old days of the Democratic monopoly or even back in the era of the county unit system and rural courthouse control of the General Assembly.

At least we didn't expect much better—and we knew precisely whom to blame.

Time to Untie the Hands
of the FBI?

Syndicated column—April 26, 1995

Speaker Newt Gingrich proposes restoring the FBI's once-broad authority to infiltrate domestic terrorist organizations. The idea makes sense, but it should be approached with care.

A tip from a paid FBI informant might have prevented the Oklahoma City bombing. We can never know for sure.

What we do know is this: Violence in the South in the 1960s was limited because FBI spies permeated the ranks of the Ku Klux Klan and similar racist groups.

To be sure, there were still outrages. The church bombings in Alabama, the murder of Col. Lemuel Penn in Georgia, the killing of three civil rights workers in Mississippi—all were the work of organized hatemongers.

Still, violence in the South would have been much more pervasive if the FBI and other law-enforcement agencies had operated under presently severe restrictions on surveillance. Without adequate FBI intelligence and the ability to take pre-emptive action, the South of the mid-1960s might have been embroiled in guerrilla warfare.

As it was, the power of the Ku Klux Klan virtually evaporated after Georgia Congressman Charles Weltner conducted extensive hearings on the Klan in 1965-66.

The House hearings revealed the Klan as an organization that spawned terror, purchased firearms, planned bombings, and cheated its members out of money. Weltner relied on FBI intelligence reports to turn the spotlight on the KKK, which was fatally wounded by the public exposure.

I recall once being led blindfolded to a secret Klan initiation ceremony in which all participants wore hoods and masks. When I suggested to my Klansman escort that an innocent newspaper reporter might get hurt in such an environment, he said reassuringly: "Don't worry. Half these guys are on the FBI's payroll." (So was he, as it turned out.)

In retrospect, I believe undercover FBI agents wrecked the Ku Klux Klan, although they never received credit.

In the late 1960s, public sentiment, fueled by increasingly liberal media, turned against federal law-enforcement agencies. FBI Director J. Edgar Hoover was depicted as a tyrannical sex pervert who used his power to blackmail public officials. The FBI was made out to be an organization of brutes and Peeping Toms.

Even if it had been OK to penetrate the KKK and the White Citizens Council, it certainly was not all right to spy on anti-war groups, some of whom had allied themselves with our enemies. At least that became the prevailing opinion of the time.

Hoover's demise and Richard Nixon's rise and fall left the FBI in shambles. First the administration of President Gerald Ford and then the Carter White House moved to restrict the FBI's intelligence-gathering activities and stop the agency's perceived abuses.

We are in the midst of a new era of terrorism, except it is more intense than any we experienced in the 1960s and 1970s. Our borders are virtually defenseless against throngs of aliens wishing to settle here. Their numbers increasingly include fanatics bent on destroying the nation.

Domestic hate groups—white supremacists, black supremacists, and just plain lunatics—are proliferating. All seem to have one thing in common: They despise the government and will go to any lengths to bring it down. Several of these paramilitary cells, centered mostly in the West and Midwest, are larger, better-equipped, and more highly motivated than any KKK klavern ever hoped to be.

The suggestion to give the FBI more authority to collect intelligence is probably overdue.

A word of caution is in order. Increasing the intelligence-gathering capacity of police agencies invariably leads to infringements on freedoms. We also must be certain that criticism of the government and legitimate protests are never treated as unlawful acts.

During the Carter years, Attorney General Griffin Bell tinkered with a new charter for the FBI to try to give fresh direction to the bureau and rebuild its morale. "We looked on it as an exhaustive attempt to protect citizens' liberties from unjustified invasions by FBI agents without sacrificing citizens' security by shackling agents so tightly they could not do their jobs," Bell wrote in his memoirs, *Taking Care of the Law.*

The new-charter idea fizzled after Bell departed Washington. Perhaps the time is ripe for another Georgian, Newt Gingrich, to reopen the discussion with a bit more emphasis on "citizens' security."

On Criticism of the Media

Syndicated column — April 30, 1995

The hand-wringing and finger-pointing are close to getting out of hand.

Jimmy Carter has joined President Bill Clinton in suggesting radio talk-show hosts share blame for the Oklahoma City bombing. The broadcast personalities should tone down their criticism of public officials, says the former president.

"To condemn the government as a threat to our liberty or as a disgrace to the principles of America is completely wrong," Carter said in a speech in Plains.

On another front, House Speaker Newt Gingrich has jumped with both feet on the news media. He called a newspaper report on his balanced-budget plan "maniacally stupid." He said *The New York Times* has "become a joke" and asserted that political reporters "run around looking for people to bite."

Clinton, Gingrich, and Carter have little in common, except an overwhelming ambition to be loved universally and a strong distaste for criticism.

The freedom to speak out, to dissent, to chastise public officials — those are among the things that make this republic magnificent and worth preserving.

Beware politicians who would use catastrophe to try to quash public disapproval and discourse.

To be sure, the media — Rush Limbaugh as well as *The New York Times* — ought to expect to get punched back when they lambast Clinton, Carter, Gingrich or anybody else.

But even a faint hint of a need for censorship is way out of bounds.

If there is fault with the media, it is not in inspiring mad bombers or even in making light of Speaker Newt's "Contract With America." It is, instead, in pandering to popular sentiment and not reporting well enough — or even critically enough — on government.

In recent days, radio, TV, and newspapers have given us spectacular coverage of the Oklahoma tragedy. Before that, they saturated us with details of the O.J. Simpson murder trial.

The media have covered extensively the words and persona of Speaker Newt. Yet we have examined him mostly as if he were a bug in a bottle, a curiosity with a white mane. We have seldom scrutinized him as a revolutionary and an architect of profound change. Such an examination might be painfully boring and could never compete with O.J. for viewers and readers.

The media are getting better and better at covering interesting and visually sensational events, but we may be ignoring the trends that shape our destiny.

For instance, Sen. Paul Coverdell of Georgia, an emerging power in Washington, recently called for Mexico, Colombia, Peru, and Bolivia to come to the conference table to stop the flood of drugs pouring into this country.

"There is no other threat that more seriously challenges the national security of the United States and this hemisphere than the drug cartel," Coverdell said. "In the United States, drug availability and purity of cocaine and heroin are at an all-time high. ... Approximately 2.5 percent of all live births in this country are now cocaine- or crack-exposed babies.

"The drug cartel ships hundreds of tons of cocaine into the United States, killing and maiming more Americans each year than died in all of the years of our engagement in Vietnam. If another country were pouring chemicals into the United States causing the death and maiming of tens of thousands of citizens, it would not be tolerated. The whole nation would rise up in defense. And yet, we are quietly proceeding without attacking the problem," Coverdell declared.

The drug problem is old hat and hard to photograph. Coverdell speaks too softly and is not particularly photogenic. Besides, Judge Lance Ito was on his way back to the bench.

So, We The Media ignored the senator's call for a hemispheric parley and his warning of approaching disaster. For that, we deserve the harshest criticism.

The End of Two-Party Politics

Syndicated column—September 6, 1995

Is the era of two-party politics over? Are our national and state governments about to enter a period when the Democratic and Republican parties will represent just two of several sturdy political persuasions competing for power? Or is one of the traditional parties, probably the Democratic one, about to disappear from the public scope?

There is not much doubt that a seismic political shift is in the making. Retired Gen. Colin Powell, a hero of Eisenhower dimensions, is said to be considering a presidential bid as an independent candidate. Sen. Bill Bradley of New Jersey, an energetic centrist Democrat, is retiring from the Senate. He declares the policies of both Democrats and Republicans are unsatisfactory, and he hints strongly that he will run for the presidency as a third-party alternative.

Sen. Sam Nunn is thinking of quitting the Senate because he no longer fits into the Democratic Party and cannot bring himself to turn Republican.

In Georgia, Rep. Tyrone Brooks, president of the Georgia Association of Black Elected Officials, says he is prepared to lead formation of a third party of African Americans to join forces with the Rev. Jesse Jackson's Rainbow Coalition. Black Georgians will leave the Democrats if the Legislature fails to give them more than one majority-black congressional district, Brooks says.

(A wholesale defection of black voters would be fatal to the Democratic Party.)

Ten days ago, a third of the state House Republican Caucus broke ranks with the GOP and voted with Democratic House Speaker Tom Murphy on a redistricting plan. That incident is important only because it demonstrates a breakdown of party discipline.

Rigid two-party distinctions may have ended some time ago. They began to disintegrate when candidates discovered the power of TV advertising and precise polling techniques. The party label's importance diminished. Party primaries, often controlled by extremists, have become hindrances to ambition for high office. Candidates often must adopt positions in primaries that are anathema to a more moderate electorate in general elections. (In the 1994 GOP primary, gubernatorial candidate Guy Millner opposed the state lottery, then tried to disavow that opposition in the general election campaign. His first stance helped him win the nomination but may have cost him the election.)

A glimpse at the recent behavior of some of our most celebrated partisan figures shows clearly how party lines have become blurred. For instance:

—Sen. Nunn, a lifelong Democrat, compiled a voting record more favorable than nearly any other senator's to the policies of Republican President Ronald Reagan. Nunn has been a reluctant, sometimes downright sullen, supporter of the Democratic presidential ticket in recent times.

—Gov. Zell Miller, once the champion of minorities and the labor movement, now sounds more Republican than most Republicans. Public-opinion polls suggest voters want welfare reform, punitive prison sentences, and fewer government programs. Those are ideals first espoused by Republican leaders, now fully embraced by one-time liberal Gov. Miller.

—Attorney General Mike Bowers quit the Democratic Party and joined the GOP last year with great fanfare, declaring he no longer felt comfortable as a Democrat. However, Bowers remains more closely allied with the Democratic Miller administration than with his newfound friends among Republicans. When Miller needed a legal cover for his veto of a reduction in property taxes, Bowers furnished him an official opinion supporting his position. When Bowers needed a powerful plaintiff to join in a lawsuit against fellow Republican Insurance Commissioner John Oxendine, Miller obliged.

Until the 1960s, most Southerners thought of the Democratic Party in terms of the New Deal and help for the farmers and veterans. A broad band of racism also ran through the populist policies of Southern Democratic leaders.

Wall Street, the Great Depression, and carpetbaggers were the images and legacies of the GOP.

Now the Democratic Party is viewed by many as the party of militant minorities, oppressive taxation, and vacillating foreign policies. The modern Republican Party is often seen as too pious and mean-spirited and lacking diversity. There is little middle ground left in either the Democrat or Republican ideology.

Few modern politicians relish association with extremes. So it's no wonder the two-party system seems to be unraveling.

The Olympics: One Year Out

Syndicated column—July 16, 1995

The Olympic dormitories are mysteriously settling into the ground. The Olympic coins are not selling well. Neither are the commemorative bricks. The Atlanta Games are presently $112 million in the red. There are labor troubles brewing in the private security force. The agriculture commissioner says he's worried about equine disease in the Olympic show horses. Not nearly enough hotel rooms are available. The weather is hot, hot, hot. And the traffic is terrible. ...

Ever wonder what Billy Payne thinks when he wakes every morning? Does the Grand Master of the Atlanta Olympics ask himself: "Why did I get into this?" Does he turn on the radio first thing to get the word on the Olympic crisis of the day?

Probably both of the above. But the fellow who brought the '96 Games to Atlanta seems not to notice the axe is about to fall. He puts on his most optimistic public face and promises over and over that good things will come from the Olympics.

On Wednesday, the Atlanta Games will mark one year and counting until the torch is brought into the new stadium to signal the beginning of the Centennial events.

So perhaps it is time to put aside for a moment those dark headlines. To forget about the gay controversy that kept a major venue from going to Cobb County. To suspend memories of Atlanta Mayor Bill Campbell's successful drive to scuttle Olympic golf in Augusta.

Those are niggling, fading episodes. The fact is, the 1996 Olympics can turn out to be the most significant 17 days in the state's history.

The Olympiad will pump an estimated $5.1 billion into Georgia's economy and spin off 80,000 jobs, according to a new University of Georgia study.

The Games will focus worldwide attention on Atlanta, Savannah, Columbus, Augusta, and the rest of the state. Even Birmingham, Ala., will share the spotlight.

In examining the everyday problems of preparing for the Games, we may overlook the big picture.

We need reminding: The 1996 Olympic Games will be the largest peacetime gathering of sports competitors in the annals of the world.

More than 10,000 athletes from nearly 200 countries are expected to participate.

The Atlanta Olympics will dwarf, by comparison, the recent Games in Barcelona and Los Angeles.

Millions of visitors will pour into Atlanta and Georgia. Organizers of the '96 Games expect to sell more tickets than the directors of any other Olympics ever dreamed of peddling: At least 11 million tickets will be sold to events across the state.

The Games will be more than a giant track-and-field meet. They will provide a showcase for high technology and 21st century communications. They will create an opportunity to prove that Southern hospitality is more than a myth.

They will test local and state government's ability to control traffic and provide security. They can show the world the falsity of the Forrest Gump-Snuffy Smith-KKK stereotype of the Southern region of the United States.

When Atlanta and Georgia were first chosen for the '96 Games, many fretted that too many public resources might be invested. Now, some worry that too little might be expended to assure the success of the Games.

State government has already pumped at least $200 million into Olympics-related enterprises, ranging from housing and swimming pools to improved highways and marine facilities.

As the deadline for preparations approaches, government is bound to spend more on the Games, including premium payments for hurry-up last-minute projects.

If the UGA economic forecasts are even close, history will say those public investments were wise.

Back to the bad news: Each time another potential catastrophe (e.g., tilting buildings, sick horses, inflated prices) crops up for the Olympics, Billy Payne is not the only guy on the spot. We all are.

Hey, Newt, Remember Bert?

AT&T Interchange — December 7, 1995

At first, Newt Gingrich and his staff appeared pleased and relieved. At least that was the impression they tried to give.

The speaker of the House contended he had prevailed in his running battle against charges of impropriety. After 13 months of deliberation, the House Ethics Committee had tossed out all but one of the 65 charges of wrongdoing against Gingrich.

The single count was based on a "limited technical point," says Gingrich. It related to whether a tax-exempt foundation was used to finance a politically partisan college course taught by the speaker. A special counsel will delve into the matter.

Gingrich's lawyers analyzed the accusation and said it will be nearly impossible to prove. They may be right. Several legal authorities who don't care for Gingrich also say it's a bum rap.

Worse still for Newt's detractors, the surviving charge won't fit on a bumper sticker. So it can't be used as a handy political club to knock Newt around and amuse voters. No one, except some tax accountants, fully understands the allegation.

Whew! sighs Gingrich. That was close, but it'll soon be over.

"I am confident the remaining charge will be dismissed," said the speaker. "This has been a very painful process for my wife, my family, and me personally."

Hold the phone. It is not over. This may be only the beginning.

The opening scenes of The Trial of the Speaker are nearly a copy of the first act of the slow-moving drama that finally brought down another Georgian in Washington nearly 20 years ago.

Remember Bert Lance? He was the affable Georgia banker who came to Washington in 1977 as President Jimmy Carter's budget director. Lance was easily the best-liked, most accessible member of the Carter team. Oh, there were a few questions about his taxes and disposal of some bank shares back in Georgia.

The problems seemed small and complicated, and no one paid much attention at first. Lance and Carter dismissed out of hand their importance. Then there were new allegations, and they weren't quite so complex. And then there were more. And still more.

A Senate investigation was launched. The Justice Department got involved. Soon, poor Lance was spending all his time defending himself against a growing avalanche of claims.

Finally, he threw in the towel. He resigned because, he said, he was too busy fending off would-be prosecutors to serve President Carter.

A year later, he was indicted, tried, and acquitted on dozens of criminal counts growing out of his financial dealings. Although he was cleared, his public career was destroyed. Once a leading candidate for governor of Georgia, Lance nearly dropped from sight and never held a government office again.

Lance and Gingrich are not kindred souls. Lance was the key to making the Carter administration work. He knew how to get along with the Democratic Congress and how to defuse controversies. Some believe that if Lance had survived to advise Carter in the final year of his administration, the Carter presidency might have lasted another four years.

Gingrich is the antithesis of Lance—a controversial firebrand.

But is Speaker Newt treading the same path as Lance?

He has clearly won the first round of his ethics battle. The most serious imputations have been rejected.

Round two is about to begin. House Minority Leader David Bonior, D-Mich., is bringing new ethics charges. He accuses the speaker of improperly using at least $250,000 from his GOPAC fund for his 1990 congressional campaign. The Federal Election Commission has leveled the same accusation.

That allegation opens new avenues of investigation. Exactly who are GOPAC's major contributors, and why has Speaker Newt kept them secret for all these years? And precisely what is GOPAC, and how were its funds used to promote the ideas, ideals, and perhaps even the lifestyle of the conservative congressman from Georgia?

We may never get the answers to those questions. Yet they will be propounded repeatedly in the coming months. An investigative feeding frenzy will develop around the speaker's doorstep. Everywhere he turns, he will face another question, another accusation, and perhaps another subpoena.

For the past year, Gingrich has been the shooting star of American politics, living in the glow of the public spotlight and loving every minute of it. Now the glare will begin to hurt.

Back in Gingrich's home district, some old-timers will bet even money that Newt will be out of politics a year from now. They say Gingrich will be nibbled into political oblivion, in much the same way the kinder, gentler Bert Lance was driven from public life. The lightning-rod revolution-maker may have become a burden too heavy for his Republican revolutionaries to carry.

Agents for change often don't last long. In Gingrich's case, the status quo in Washington rose against him as soon as he ascended to power. Gingrich could do no right: He said the wrong things; his book deals looked rotten; his family was not a fit; he was cold-hearted and cruel. That's what they said anyway.

None of that may be true. Yet, in the end, Gingrich played into the hands of his enemies. He talked too much. He was drawn to TV appearances as a moth is to flame.

If his Republican colleagues decide he cannot continue to lead them, Gingrich and the country may have lost an opportunity to embrace genuine changes in government policy. If that gate, which Gingrich opened, closes, the speaker himself will be most responsible.

Bye-Bye To A Bad Year

AT&T Interchange – December 27, 1995

This was not a very good year. The significant news of 1995 was mostly grim. Not much of it was inspiring.

We sent no astronauts to the moon. We eradicated no killing diseases. We did not settle a major global confrontation. We made no giant strides toward ending poverty, violence, and ignorance.

We did those things in other years, not in 1995.

This was The Year of the Newt, The O. J. Annum, and The Time of the Quitters. If we discovered anything in 1995, it was that the nation seems out of focus and perhaps mean-spirited.

Time magazine chose Newt Gingrich as its Man of the Year. Gingrich and 1995 are a good fit.

The speaker of the House began the year as the leader of a grand revolution that he promised would change America forever. Gingrich would lead the way to lower taxes, less government, and more freedom.

As the year closed, Gingrich was trying his best to keep a lower profile and avoid further embarrassment to himself and his followers. A special counsel was appointed to investigate charges of improper conduct brought against the speaker. The speaker burst into tears when he was told the House Ethics Committee would name an outside lawyer to inquire into his financial arrangements.

There were the first rumblings of a rebellion against Gingrich among freshman Republican representatives.

An impasse developed between Congress and the White House over a projected balanced federal budget. The government shut down twice in two months.

A dozen senators, including such lions as Bill Bradley, Sam Nunn, and Bennett Johnston, announced they would not seek re-election. Twenty-two House members called it quits. Many cited meanness and money as reasons for throwing in the towel: Too much time and effort go into raising campaign cash, and Washington has become an increasingly adversarial and angry place.

Another senator, Bob Packwood of Oregon, was forced to resign. President Clinton's popularity went up as Speaker Newt's went down.

Yet the Whitewater scandal loomed larger and could engulf Clinton before the next election.

Still, the most telling stories of 1995 occurred far outside the Washington Beltway.

The televised O. J. Simpson murder trial let millions of Americans in on a couple of dirty little secrets: Our criminal-justice system is a mess, and money and celebrity can fix nearly anything.

As the year ended, Simpson worked on an infomercial to give his opinion of the murder of his wife and her friend—a view he declined to share with the court and the jury that freed him.

The bombing of a federal building in Oklahoma City left at least 167 dead and spread shock and uneasiness across the land.

Another defining event of 1995 made headlines briefly, then disappeared: Alabama brought back chain gangs. Other states planned to follow the Alabama example.

Alabama's wardens explained that it is more efficient to shackle prisoners together when they perform hard labor. Takes fewer guards. Saves taxpayers' money. And it sends a message.

Who would have thought in, say, 1975 or 1985 that we would blithely abide chaining men while they work?

But then who would have dreamed that in 1995 we would have more than a million men and women in prisons? Or that our elected representatives would advocate measures to deprive poor children of public assistance? Or that they would endorse rationing medical care for the aged?

Nineteen ninety-five has been the "Don't Care Year." It has been a time in which the politics of moderation and compassion have waned. Intolerance of tolerance is the new style.

Surely, 1996 will be an improvement. The Centennial Olympic Games in Atlanta next summer will bring together the world's best athletes in what ought to be a magnificent demonstration of international camaraderie.

The 1996 elections will give us a chance to determine whether those stern ideologues we let take over the government this year are really what we had in mind when we chose them.

The New Year will have to be better.

Nineteen ninety-six wasn't much better. The Atlanta Olympics left much to be desired.

First, We Ban All the Cameras ...

Syndicated column—January 21, 1996

Three bills are pending in the Legislature that will restrict or even ban television coverage of the courts.

In the grand scheme of balanced budgets, tax reductions, crime rates, and teacher raises, those anti-TV bills seem trivial.

They are not. The other headline-making issues will pass. Erosions of fundamental rights, even seemingly minor ones, have a way of lingering and growing larger.

House Speaker Tom Murphy, D-Bremen, has offered a measure that would allow any party to a trial to veto TV coverage. Rep. Randy Sauder, R-Marietta, has proposed even tougher legislation. He would allow witnesses, as well as the judge and the opposing parties, to stop the cameras.

Even when coverage was permitted, Sauder would restrict to five minutes the amount of time a newscast could devote to a televised trial.

That is akin to having a law which would tell a newspaper editor he could allocate no more than six column inches to a county commission meeting. This is Alice-in-Wonderland stuff. But it could become law. What Murphy wants, Murphy usually gets. Whether the speaker wants to go as far as young Sauder remains to be seen.

Murphy and Sauder's ideas grew out of the public outrage at the O.J. Simpson murder trial. That months-long, real-life TV drama finally let the American public in on the bad news that Justice may be not only blind—she is corruptible as well.

Was that the fault of television? The lawmakers say it was. They contend lawyers, judges, witnesses, and even jurors act differently when the camera is on and millions are watching.

Murphy points out that TV cameras intimidate jurors and witnesses and hinder fairness. He has a valid point. But there are a couple of other issues worth considering:

Item one: TV coverage of the courts already is restricted. In Georgia, a trial judge has the ultimate power to decide whether the cameras roll in his court. It is part of the rules of court, written by the courts. Letting the Legislature write court rules may open a door better left closed.

Suppose the courts retaliated by ordering TV crews to abandon the legislative chambers.

The ever-watchful, merciless TV devices in the state House and Senate have proved to be far more effective disciplinarians than the strictest presiding officers. In the bad old days before TV, legislators read newspapers and books and even dozed while their colleagues debated. Occasionally, a drunken lawmaker would rise to speak, only to be shouted down by his cohorts. Once in a while, a lady of the evening would wander into the legislative halls to see whether she recognized anyone. And a legislator showed up one day wearing a Roman toga. That doesn't happen anymore.

When television arrived, the horseplay ended. Legislators became attentive. The drunks and derelicts disappeared. The General Assembly is a model of decorum. TV did create one problem, however: Even after an issue has been decided, a half dozen or so lawmakers feel compelled to take the well to demonstrate their debating talents for the folks back home. If the cameras weren't there, these frustrated actors might remain silent.

Item two: Most of what happens in court is dull, and TV is not interested. An O. J. Simpson trial comes along once every 50 years or so. The Lindbergh kidnapping trial, which created a circus of grinding newsreel cameras and popping flashbulbs, resulted in a similar anti-media backlash 60 years ago.

Georgia is not La-La Land. There aren't many Judge Lance Itos presiding over our courts. Overly intrusive and abusive TV coverage of our legal system is rare, perhaps nonexistent.

To be sure, TV is a disrupting influence. Banning cameras would certainly make the courts more orderly. Come to think of it, keeping out reporters and spectators also would make our legal system more efficient.

Would Reps. Murphy and Sauder consider that also? Probably not.

The proposed ban on cameras in the courtroom failed in the Legislature.

Lingering Concerns about Olympics Security

Syndicated column—January 24, 1996

Some leading Democrats tout Billy Payne for governor. Or senator. A few well-heeled old grads believe Payne may be just the man to take over the athletic program at the University of Georgia. A half dozen law firms would certainly like to add Payne's name to their list of partners.

Though the Atlanta Olympics are still more than six months away, Payne already is hailed as a hero. His face is on the cover of *Sports Illustrated*. He is featured in dozens of interviews in the international media. He exudes confidence and optimism.

The smell of success for the Atlanta Games is in the air. Olympics chief Payne rightly deserves credit for attracting the Games to Georgia and focusing the attention of the world on our region for 17 days this summer.

To be sure, the Olympics have a down side. The Games undoubtedly will cause massive traffic jams, prolonged inconveniences, disruption of the primary elections, price gouging, ambush marketing, hidden taxpayer costs, and on and on. The national press will discover for the umpteenth time impoverished families living within a few blocks of the Georgia Capitol. Still, these are minor annoyances compared to the good things that should spring from the Games.

The Games will be great for the state. They will generate hundreds of millions of dollars. They will burnish our image and give us a running start into the next millennium.

There is one nagging matter, however, that could turn those splendid days in July and August into disaster—a breakdown in security.

A wave of violent crime, uncontrollable civil disobedience, an unspeakable act of terrorism—those are the night frights for Olympics planners.

A public-safety failure could ruin the 1996 Games and taint our reputation for 50 years.

There is good reason for concern. Some believe the Atlanta Police Department is not prepared to carry out its part in keeping order. The

151

Atlanta police have been caught up in a months-long series of scandals. Morale is low, and esprit de corps has all but disappeared.

With less than 170 days before the Games, state government has reorganized its security brass. Gov. Zell Miller has relieved State Patrol Col. Stock Coleman of his post as coordinator of state security for the Games.

He has appointed GBI director Buddy Nix, Public Safety Commissioner Sid Miles, and Adjutant General William Bland to a newly formed executive board to oversee security. He has named Georgia Emergency Management chief Gary McConnell as Coleman's successor and executive director of state security for the Olympics.

Reasons for this sudden shakeup are not clear. Coleman is an old hand at dealing with large-scale security projects. He was Gov. Jimmy Carter's security chief and a leader in law enforcement for the 1988 Democratic Convention in Atlanta.

However, federal officials, including Vice President Al Gore, have expressed concern about planning for the complex public-safety problems associated with the Games. A Capitol source said Coleman was "too inflexible" in his dealings with other law enforcement agencies. McConnell, a former sheriff, has directed emergency relief from a number of natural disasters since he joined the Miller administration. McConnell generally gets high marks from federal agencies.

Gov. Miller has allocated about $30 million for housing, food, and specialized training for nearly 2,000 Georgia lawmen who will join federal and local forces in policing the Olympics.

Hundreds of private security agents will be employed. Federal agents are likely to play the most significant, though least noticed, role in assuring tranquility for the Games.

Of all the problems facing the Olympics organizers, none are more delicate than those associated with safety and order.

Law-enforcement agencies must be certain millions of visitors are protected in a city that was recently cited as the most violent in the country.

At the same time, their efforts must not be so obtrusive as to distract from the Games or create a police-state atmosphere.

In the end, security may be the most important item on the Olympics agenda. If nothing goes wrong, it will not be mentioned after the Games. But if security fails, the dream of the Atlanta Games could turn into a nightmare.

And it did.

Why Don't We Ask *Why?*

Georgia Trend — February 1996

Hardly anyone asks *why?* anymore. In the age of 10-second sound bites, virulently partisan talk radio and bumper-sticker news, the most essential question in journalism, *why?*, has fallen through the cracks.

Of the Five Great Ws and the H—*who? what? when? where? why? and how?*—*why* used to be essential. Now it is given short shrift. The *why* is too hard to answer, often too time-consuming, sometimes too dull. Let's get on with the interesting stuff. Nowadays, we seem ready to settle for the most cursory and sometimes flat-out false explanations of public events.

More than ever, we know the *who* in the day's news—Hillary and Bill Clinton, Newt Gingrich, the Serbs, the Croats, Zell Miller, Tom Murphy, etc.

And the *what*—The Deficit, the Whitewater Scandal. Privatizing, downsizing, upgrading.

And the *when* and *where*—Feb. 12 in Iowa, Feb. 20 in New Hampshire, March 5 in Georgia, seven years for the budget in Washington, 40 days for the General Assembly in Atlanta, and 150-plus days before the Olympics.

We learn a little about the *how*—cutting spending, landing troops, appointing a special counsel, convening a federal grand jury, adjourning the Congress, holding an election.

But what about *why?*

We hear repeatedly: "The federal budget must be balanced in seven years."

Why? Why is it so important to balance the budget in seven years?

Many of the muckety-mucks who shut down the government in the gridlock over the budget won't even be around in 2003. No one knows what's going to happen between now and the magic day in the next millennium when the federal budget is to be balanced. Consider what has occurred in the past seven years.

In 1989, the Soviet Union was still a menace. Desert Storm had not occurred. Bosnia—where/what is that? Newt Gingrich was a barely surviving third-tier Republican congressman. Speaker of the U.S. House of Representatives—Newt? Get serious.

In Georgia, Lt. Gov. Zell Miller had signed off on the largest tax increase in the state's history. And Bill Clinton, the Arkansas windbag, for president? Are you kidding? No way—not after that performance at the 1988 Democratic Convention.

The nation and state were on the edge of deep recession.

We'll look back on 1996 the same way we view 1989. It will be another age. In 2003, my guess is we'll be dealing with a fresh set of problems, and government spending will not be the most compelling one.

So why have our elected leaders gone nuts over the idea of balancing the budget in seven years?

They'll tell you we must reduce the federal deficit. That sounds good. It still doesn't answer the question.

Be persistent. Ask *why* again.

There is no deficit crisis. The federal deficit is shrinking. It has fallen from 5 percent of our gross national income in 1992 to just 2.2 percent now. As a percentage of the national budget, the U.S. deficit is the smallest of the world's seven leading nations.

So why is balancing the budget in 2003 so vital? Is it because most of us want and need a tax cut? Or because the Republican Congress has no other sizzling issue for the 1996 election campaigns? Or because a TV news editor in New York can't find anything more intriguing to lead off the day's news?

The seven-year balanced budget is not the only baffler bouncing around these days. There are scores of other unsatisfactorily answered questions on public issues. Here are a few:

• Why don't we have more nuclear power plants? Nuclear power is cheaper, cleaner, and safer than energy generated by coal, oil, and gas. The anti-nuke crowd scared us to death 10 or 15 years ago about the not-quite-defined hazards of generating atomic energy. Yet the fact remains, fossil fuels kill more people directly and indirectly in a day than nuclear energy has destroyed in its entire history. You don't ever hear anyone say we should ban coal, oil, or gas.

• Why don't we hear anything these days about how acid rain is wilting our Southern forests? Is it because the threat no longer exists? Or because there was never a threat in the first place?

• Why did we send troops to Bosnia? To protect our position as the leader of NATO, they tell us.

• Why is it so critical that we protect our position as the leader of NATO? NATO was organized to guard us against invasion by the Soviet bloc. The Soviet bloc no longer exists. So what's so pressing about NATO?

And closer to home:

• Why does our government subsidize tobacco and, at the same time, declare tobacco is an addictive poison that is annihilating us by the millions?

• Why do we build cars that will easily run 110 mph, then spend days debating whether to raise the speed limit to 70 mph?

• Why does our governor demand the state abolish employment protection for 65,000 low-level public employees, but never utter a critical word about curbing the abuses inherent in granting lifetime jobs to the state's college professors?

• Why do we concentrate law enforcement efforts on arresting suppliers when the obvious, less expensive way to solve the drug problem is to target consumers? Dry up the market and the dealers will vanish, right? It's not a police solution; it's an economic one.

• Why does our state have the most lax gun laws in the country when our capital city ranks, year after year, as the most violent city in the nation?

• Why does our Legislature take just four days to remove the sales tax on food, then consider allowing local governments to add the tax back?

• Why does our state government sanction and promote gambling for itself, but will not consider allowing others to engage in gaming, even when they would create a productive industry (as in breeding horses)?

• Why are our state laws rigged so that some officials who are fired get more generous pension benefits than others who remain on the job until retirement?

• Why don't we demand immediate limits on campaign spending when it is evident that special-interest money will soon destroy our form of government?

• Why does our government tolerate pouring millions of gallons of untreated filth into our rivers? Why has our state government suddenly decided our barely enforced environmental laws are too strict?

Reasonable and complete answers to all these questions may exist, but I have not read them. In this age of information shock, we receive so much data daily that we cannot begin to absorb the meaningful *whats*, much less consider the real *whys*.

When we blend into this roiling tide of information the great herds of obfuscators (lawyers, spin doctors, public relations consultants, advertising mavens), it is no wonder we seldom understand or even ask *why*.

Dear Sam Nunn

AT&T Interchange — May 16, 1996

Memo To: The Georgia Giant, Sen. Sam Nunn
Re: Your Campaign Against Silliness

Back here in Atlanta, we're really pleased to see you speaking out on important matters again, Sam. We thought for a while you had decided to stop making public declarations since you announced you were retiring from the Senate.

We were delighted with your statement that the Republican plan for a gasoline tax rollback is "a silly idea" that won't help consumers a bit.

As usual, you're right. You deserve a round of applause from every good Southern Democrat for speaking out against such nonsense as repealing a tax on gasoline.

I hope this is just the beginning of your crusade against Republicans with silly notions. It's something you could continue with even more vigor once you leave office and no longer have to swap votes in the Senate with those fellows.

Let me suggest another easy target: Sen. John McCain, the Arizona Republican war hero, has the idea that the Defense Department is spending millions of dollars on the Olympic Games on stuff that has nothing to do with defense or national security.

That is foolish talk, Sam. You should take McCain aside and speak reasonably to him about his views. Maybe even offer him a set of Olympics pins or an Izzy doll to show him how wonderful the Olympics will be. After all, next to you, McCain is considered the most knowledgeable senator in Washington on Pentagon matters. McCain will listen to you. He doesn't want to be silly like some of those other Republicans.

On April 24, McCain and several lesser GOP lights in the Senate wrote a letter to the Pentagon declaring: "It is readily apparent from information provided by the Department of Defense that defense funds have been expended for certain activities that were not related to security at the Olympics."

He listed some nonsecurity items: publication of a special events training book, building a water system for field hockey, operating barges at Savannah.

"We are outraged that the Department would spend scarce defense resources for these types of activities," Sen. McCain wrote.

And there was more:

"We again must take exception to the following planned expenditures which do not meet the definition of security support:

" —$1.4 million to pay military personnel to drive buses and vans for Olympic athletes, including $100,000 to purchase commercial drivers licenses, and

" —$2.8 million to pay expenses which the Atlanta Committee for the Olympic Games had promised to pay but later reneged, including an unspecified amount to pay a private contractor to establish a transportation management system, meals for military drivers, purchased from approved food vendors, and housing costs for military drivers.

"We find it unconscionable that the Department of Defense would agree to place highly trained, volunteer military personnel in the position of acting as drivers for Olympic athletes. We object to the State of Georgia requiring the Department of Defense to pay for this dubious privilege by charging $100,000 for commercial drivers licenses and $20 a day to rent University of Georgia dormitory rooms. In our view, these expenditures are not authorized by law. ... Instead, it appears that mismanagement and poor planning by the organizing committee have resulted in the imposition of this latest $4.2 million unfunded mandate on the federal government."

McCain said he intends to introduce legislation to require ACOG or the state of Georgia to reimburse the Defense Department for "unauthorized" use of military personnel and materiel at the Atlanta Games. He hinted that Olympic officials expect to reap huge bonuses after the Games and suggested some of that dough could go toward paying for use of the soldiers.

Can you imagine, Sam, having to pay the federal government for using GIs as chauffeurs for Olympic jocks?

Atlanta and the Olympics have enough troubles without having to fight an outbreak of silliness. The city is running behind schedule in getting ready. It also is caught up in a great debate as to whether it is No. 1 in violent crime or just No. 2. There is already grumbling about the summer heat, and this is just the middle of May. The Spartanburg, S.C., City Council has joined the list of local governments on the route of the Olympic torch relay to adopt a resolution condemning the gay lifestyle. (Just how the Olympic planners let the ceremonial torch run become entangled in fusses over homosexuality is not clear.)

So you see, Sam, we sure don't need a war hero-senator running around, writing letters using words like "outrage" and "unconscionable" and "mismanagement" in connection with the Games.

From the perspective of Sen. McCain's home in Arizona, the use of troops for the Olympics may look like government waste. From Atlanta, it looks like the highest and best use of government resources.

Sen. McCain is like you in many ways, Sam. He probably has a brilliant future in politics. But he ought to tone down his talk about the Olympics. It's worse than silly. It's downright unpatriotic, don't you agree?

Best wishes from your old buddy,

Bill S.

The Kid Crisis

Syndicated column — June 5, 1996

An infant chokes to death on a cockroach in Atlanta. And there's a march on Washington to demand the government pay more attention to children.

Georgia welfare director Michael Thurmond is invited to Washington to tell lawmakers how many mothers he has induced to go to work to get off the public dole.

And a child left alone in Atlanta drowns in a bathtub.

Those items, recently in the headlines, have become grist for the political speechwriters' mills. Saving unfortunate children and stamping out welfare gluttons have become twin goals of office-seekers — from president to probate judge. Hardly anyone has dared suggest the solution to the "children problem" is not in Washington and Atlanta. Or that the ultimate answer is not forcing welfare moms to go to work.

The government, in fact, does not have the answer. After 30 years of wallowing in "Great Society" programs, we ought to get the message: There's a problem here that government can't solve.

The difficulty is ingrained in the social order, and the symptoms show up starkly in changing demographics.

With the eyes of the world about to focus on Atlanta and the Olympics, this may not be the politically correct time to bring this up. But recently compiled statistics on our capital city give us an idea of the magnitude of the kid crisis, which is becoming a growing burden for all of us.

Professor Douglas C. Bachtel of the University of Georgia points to births to unwed mothers as the ticking time bomb that may ultimately shatter our social order. Atlanta exemplifies the national problem in microcosm.

Says Bachtel:

"The data [on the city] show that if it weren't for births to unwed mothers, the city of Atlanta's population would be in a complete nosedive."

Bachtel and his staff traced the total number of births and deaths to Atlanta mothers over a 15-year period between 1980 and 1994. The data show that white births exceeded white deaths by only 540, while black births exceeded black deaths by 51,000 over the 15-year time frame.

In 1994, Bachtel's study reveals that 59 percent of all births in the city of Atlanta were to unwed mothers. A startling 78 percent (4,684) of the black mothers who gave birth in 1994 were unwed, while 15 percent of the white mothers (348) were unwed during that same year.

Other statistics are just as appalling. Sixty-five percent of our prison population is black males. Atlanta has the highest rate of violent crime in the nation. Our rate of poverty is second only to Newark, N.J. (The metro area—the suburbs surrounding the city—is one of the most prosperous and fast-growing regions in the country. Only Las Vegas exceeds the Atlanta expanse in growth.)

The UGA professor does not draw any conclusions from his study, but he doesn't need to. The lack of cohesive, two-parent families is connected directly to the high poverty and crime numbers.

And this is not a government problem, though, to be sure, public policies may not discourage the high rate of pregnancies to unwed mothers.

Demonstrations in Washington and politically charged demands for "welfare reform" will not change a permissive culture that is dividing our society and increasing our rolls of public dependency.

Same-sex marriages seem to be the latest fad in the headlines. Turning our attention to opposite-sex marriages and stable families may be a much more important topic over the long haul.

Atlanta Mayor Bill Campbell has articulated a grand dream, "a renaissance" for Atlanta after the Olympics. Much of the business community has signed on to his plan. The mayor insists on blaming the press for many of the city's problems, including its negative image.

Some of what he says may be valid. But the answer to Atlanta's problems lies not in constructing gleaming new towers along Peachtree Street or even on the Southside. Nor will muzzling an already too timid press correct the city's ills.

The core of Atlanta's malady is found in the stark numbers on Bachtel's computer and in the thick registers of the state departments of Corrections and Human Resources and on the police blotters. Government has already proved it cannot cure the illness.

Our values must change if those numbers are to improve. And government has yet to find a way to alter the culture of dependency it helped create or make young unmarried men and women decide making babies is not an acceptable pastime.

Can the States Reform Welfare?

Syndicated column—August 7, 1996

Advocates of states' rights should celebrate. Washington is giving up. Power is flowing back to Atlanta and Montgomery and Tallahassee and Columbia.

The Democratic president and the Republican Congress are in agreement, finally. They have decided the states can do a better job, with less money, of taking care of poor people. Or not taking care of poor people.

They have stamped OK on a bill that will: (1) end the New Deal guarantee of government help for the poor, (2) finish off Lyndon Johnson's Great Society notions, and (3) force welfare bums to get off their duffs and go to work.

They're going to let the states carry out most of these missions.

Many of us were so busy being bedazzled by the Olympics that we hardly noticed. A sea change may have occurred in Washington.

Speaker Newt's Congress decided it didn't care about helping Bob Dole create issues for his presidential campaign. Instead, it tailored a Welfare Reform Bill to fit President Clinton's stated goals for changing public assistance.

President Clinton apparently decided he no longer needs to appease the bleeding-heart survivors of New Dealism in the Democratic Party. After all, they have no place else to go.

He reads the polls, knows white males are angry, and wants to do something to make them like him. He announces he will sign the welfare bill. He will end long-term public assistance to impoverished women—and their children. He will cut off help for the children of illegal aliens. He will dispatch packages of cash to the states to let them formulate their own programs for squeezing the poor.

Gov. Zell Miller must be ecstatic. For the past six years, he has endorsed the idea that the state government of Georgia could do a more efficient job of administering welfare. Could get tougher with poor people. Could make them want to straighten up and fly right.

This is the same state government that for more than a year lost track of billions of dollars in sales-tax receipts and disbursements and may not now be able to account precisely for withholding-tax payments.

And the same state that has failed to carry out federal mandates to clean up its rivers and lakes and reduce the amount of pollutants its population breathes.

And the same state that has a Medicaid program that continues to grow exponentially and has turned into an administrative nightmare.

And the same state that has an Education Department that has devolved into a battleground over political turf and not much else.

Still, Gov. Miller insists the state of Georgia and state taxpayers can do a better job in the welfare area.

(To his credit, Miller's Human Resources commissioner, Tommy Olmstead, and his Family and Children Services director, Michael Thurmond, are among the more competent administrators in state government.)

As he prepares to accept this new power from Washington, Gov. Miller may remember the bad old days of the state Department of Public Welfare. Back when the welfare rolls were purged of nearly every able-bodied person twice a year—at crop-planting time in the spring and cotton-picking time in the summer and autumn.

As soon as the crops were taken care of, the welfare checks were restored.

The federal government took over responsibility for public assistance partly because of that kind of corruption at the state level.

Gov. Miller also may recall why he was once ostracized by Georgia's conservative Democratic establishment.

Miller, then lieutenant governor, walked the streets of Atlanta handing out campaign literature for his close friend, a black liberal congressional candidate.

That candidate, now a congressman, John Lewis stood in the well of the House last week and commented on the welfare bill that the governor of Georgia hopes to help administer.

"Where is the compassion? Where is the sense of decency? Where is the heart of this Congress? This bill is mean. It is base. It is down-right low down. What does it profit a great nation to conquer the world, only to lose its soul?" cried Lewis.

Wonder what his pal Gov. Miller was thinking as Lewis pleaded.

The federal welfare bill became law. And Georgia adopted a model state-welfare system aimed at purging the rolls of recipients of public assistance.

Living and Dying
in the Red Zone

Syndicated column—November 27, 1996

There is a map of the United States floating around on the Internet that gives us a hint about our uncertain future. This official U.S. Environmental Protection Agency chart is speckled with red dots.

Southern California is covered by them; so is the industrial Northeast. So is north Georgia. We are in the red zone. Our state contains an area that has one of the worst air-pollution problems in the country. That is the meaning of the red dots.

If you live outside Georgia's red zone—in, say, parts of south Georgia—the air-pollution map may not mean much to you. Perhaps it should.

The problems of clean air and clean water could cause significant economic displacement in and around Georgia's economic engine with a statewide ripple effect. Metro Atlanta is already feeling the pain of failing to comply with the EPA's Clean Air standards.

For the first time in 40 years, there is not a single interstate highway construction project under way in the city of Atlanta.

Within the next few months, the federal money tap for new road construction in most of metro Atlanta will be shut off unless the region suddenly comes into compliance with Clean Air standards.

That is unlikely. For the problem is too pervasive. We started too late. Besides, geography and the atmosphere are against us.

The Atlanta region experiences more episodes of air inversions than any other metro area east of the Mississippi River. Stale-air pockets plus a zillion cars on our highways every day is a formula for a poisoned atmosphere. Stopping highway construction while traffic increases also is a recipe for increasing the amount of toxins we breathe.

Some state officials, including Transportation Commissioner Wayne Shackelford, have hinted air-emission standards for Georgia are unreasonable and do not take into consideration the natural peculiarities of the region.

Industrial developers have warned that unless Clean Air standards are relaxed, economic expansion in the Atlanta area may slow to a crawl.

Meanwhile, the EPA has announced it intends this week to propose a set of even tougher standards for clean air. That means that Atlanta will keep its red dot. Dozens of other Georgia communities that are now considered outside the red zone could suddenly find themselves out of compliance with the Clean Air Act.

Lest we forget, the Clean Air standards are not supposed to be imposed with economics in mind. Easier breathing, better health, and longer life are the stated goals.

Still, the new standards are almost certain to create a howl in Congress. Governors are likely to pressure their congressmen to fight the proposals.

Whether our own Speaker Newt Gingrich will be up to such a battle is uncertain. His 1994-95 opposition to tougher environmental regulations contributed significantly to his image as a national villain. He may not want to experience such vilification again.

Even if the new standards are not adopted, our capital region will remain in noncompliance. Easing the standards slightly won't help much. Our present rate of growth suggests we'd be right back in the red zone in a couple of months.

In any event, the standards, strict or easy, are not the problem. The real trouble is a lack of coordinated planning and communication among the dozen local governments in and around Atlanta.

The state has attempted to control air pollution—and, to a lesser extent, water pollution—in the Atlanta region. It has failed because too many local governments have too many different agendas and goals.

Atlanta City Hall is mainly interested in providing municipal jobs. Gwinnett County's government wants to promote growth. Cobb is caught between a wish to expand and a desire to brake further development. Poor DeKalb is trying to reverse an apparently inevitable trend toward glut and urbanization. So it goes.

There is little guidance emanating from the Statehouse. Gov. Zell Miller sidesteps the issue of consolidation of planning and services. House Majority Leader Larry Walker, D-Perry, has made a few tentative steps to encourage local-government mergers.

The notion of consolidating government services does not sit well with influential City Hall and county courthouse lobbies in the Capitol.

Meanwhile, the problems grow worse. Planners tell us if a coordinated solution to our pollution problems is not found soon, Georgia's wave of prosperity will ebb. Commercial growth will shift elsewhere, to Charlotte and Raleigh-Durham and Jacksonville and other venues that are not designated by red dots on the pollution map.

Riddles from the General Assembly

Syndicated column—January 12, 1997

What do welfare mothers, poor kids, and hardened convicts have in common?

a. They have little political influence.

b. They will be principal topics of discussion in the 1997 Legislature.

c. They will be used to help elect the next governor.

d. All of the above.

If you answered "d," go to the head of the class or to the "will call" booth in the Gold Dome. You are entitled to a free ticket to the Monday opening of the Georgia General Assembly.

To be sure, more pressing issues will come before the new legislative session.

Few will be mentioned more frequently than Work First, Gov. Zell Miller's universally applauded plan to force welfare mothers off the public dole and into the work force.

It is a splendid idea, adopted by President Bill Clinton, endorsed by challenger Bob Dole, and espoused by numerous Republicans and Democrats in the 1996 election campaigns.

The Christian Coalition, not always on Gov. Miller's side, has issued a public pronouncement commending Miller's Work First strategy and promising to help implement it.

The only problem with this wonderful notion: Many welfare recipients are not equipped for gainful employment. The numbers of the unemployable will grow as jobs become more specialized and require increasing cognitive skills.

There is another uncomfortable question attached to Work First: In this affluent and civilized society, why are we hell-bent on penalizing children for the sins or misfortunes of their impoverished mothers? When the mothers are kicked off relief, so are their kids.

Let's leave the answer to that riddle to the bleeding hearts. You and I have more pressing governmental matters to ponder. Like what to do with 35,000 inmates languishing in Georgia prisons—and those who will follow them.

Lt. Gov. Pierre Howard, an announced candidate for governor in 1998, has the solution: Make 'em serve 100 percent of their sentences.

Also, establish a commission to "restore consistency and certainty" to the criminal justice system.

"We are going to tell the truth to Georgia criminals," said Mr. Howard. "And the truth is: If you deserve the sentence, then you are going to serve the sentence."

The lieutenant governor unveiled his plan at a state Chamber of Commerce breakfast last week. It was warmly received. He said he would introduce a bill in the Legislature to make sure bad actors in Georgia get their just desserts.

This comes from a fellow who in past years has fretted most in public about how old folks in nursing homes were treated or whether infants were receiving proper nutrition.

The new Pierre has more important and politically popular ideas to espouse. Kinder and gentler are out. Macho is in. Howard is determined to take the public-safety issue away from Republicans—and upstage Attorney General Michael Bowers, an unannounced candidate for governor.

Last year, you may recall, Bowers and his GOP friends in the Legislature introduced a bill that would require certain categories of violent felons to serve at least 85 percent of their prison sentences.

Democrats howled with anguish and derision. It couldn't be done, they cried; it would cost the state far too much. Democrats smothered the "85-percent solution" in a House committee and refused to let it be aired publicly. Republican candidates used, with mixed success, the bill and its demise as campaign issues last fall.

GOP lawmakers are back this year with a similar measure, but it is pallid stuff compared to Howard's hard-ball scheme to make all crooks and thugs serve all their hard time.

If Howard's fellow Democrats refused to give a sympathetic ear to the Bowers/GOP sentencing bill in 1996, how will they greet the lieutenant governor's more stringent proposal in 1997?

One other puzzler in our political science quiz this week: Pick the word that might best describe some of the leading personalities in the coming session of the Legislature. If you chose "posturing," you'll be eligible for a free visit to see the stuffed two-headed snake on the fourth floor of the Capitol.

The Right to Life — or Liberty

Syndicated column — January 22, 1997

Life for many of us near the end of the 20th century has turned out just fine. The economy is growing. No major war is in sight. Our health-care and higher-education systems are the best in the world. Our public schools are improving. We swim in abundance and affluence.

Small wonder that President Bill Clinton gave such an upbeat inaugural address. Gov. Zell Miller has pronounced the state of the state excellent. The prospects for Georgia and Georgians were never better.

The biggest controversy in the Legislature involves Democrats writing arcane procedural rules that Republicans complain are unfair. And, oh, yes, some conservative lawmakers are making a fuss over a new law requiring Georgians to submit to fingerprinting when they get drivers licenses. That won't amount to much.

It may be a wonderful world all right, but a couple of waves in this sea of optimism make one slightly uneasy.

Two bombs were set off last week at an abortion clinic in north Atlanta.

On Sunday, two more bombs exploded at an abortion clinic in Tulsa, Okla. Both the Atlanta and Tulsa clinics had been fire-bombed previously.

Some observers speculated the clinic bombs were connected to the Jan. 22 anniversary of Roe v. Wade, the Supreme Court ruling that legalized abortions.

Some feared the blasts might signal a wave of terrorism. If so, fellow Americans, prepare to relinquish a few more of your freedoms.

Fingerprints on your drivers licenses may be the least of your concerns.

Given a choice between safety and liberty, Georgians, like most other Americans, will opt for safety, says Georgia Attorney General Mike Bowers.

There is ample evidence to prove his point.

Some years ago, we waived our Fourth Amendment rights to unwarranted searches every time we board an airplane. That abridgment of freedom was enacted to stop airline hijacking. It has worked.

Each time we withdraw money from an ATM, a television camera records our every move. Money-machine bandits forced upon us that invasion of privacy.

When we enter a government building, we are told to empty our pockets and open our pocketbooks and briefcases. Guards scan us with metal detectors and X-ray units. We can thank violence-prone loonies and sundry anarchists for that inconvenience.

When we buy a target pistol or any other handgun, our name is fed into a computer to determine whether we are a felon or a psychotic. An attempt on the life of President Reagan wrought that invasion of our past.

Even when we log onto the Internet, an unseen authority is equipped to identify us by name and address and trace our every movement through cyberspace. Laws governing our rights to privacy in that murky area are just beginning to surface. Cyber-crooks already abound. In the end, even as technology improves, we will have less, not more, freedom to surf the Net.

A Georgia congressman, Bob Barr, has championed our freedom to buy bomb-making materials without identifying markers. He has succeeded so far in keeping ID tracers out of blasting powder. Finally, he will lose. I suspect most of us—at least those of us not into making bombs—would prefer that explosives carry identifying markers from the manufacturers.

If blasting materials were marked, we might now know the identity of Atlanta's Centennial Park terrorist. The bombers of the clinics might have been reluctant to carry out their double-barreled attacks.

Keep an eye on these random acts of terror against innocent citizens. Our police are not very good at tracking down the doers of such evil deeds. Law enforcement agencies lack adequate tools. Among the tools they say they need are more legal ways to pry into our lives.

The end of this century could be remembered as much for a loss of basic freedoms as for the good life. Let's hope not.

The Rage against Fingerprinting

Syndicated column—March 2, 1997

Try explaining this to a class of new citizens:
The 1997 session of the Georgia General Assembly is dedicated to giving criminals the harshest punishment available under our constitution. The lawmakers are proposing violent felons serve 100 percent of their sentences without hope of parole. They demand mandatory jail time for drunk drivers. They would put 10-year-old delinquents into boot camps. They would seize the assets of fathers who do not make child-support payments. Some lawmakers propose swapping the electric chair for the lethal needle so we will execute more criminals.

Paradoxically, many of the same punitive-minded legislators are determined to make it more difficult to apprehend the criminals they are so eager to discipline. At least five bills have been introduced in the House and Senate to repeal the requirement that citizens submit to fingerprinting when they receive drivers licenses.

Col. Sid Miles, Georgia Public Safety commissioner, calls drivers license fingerprinting "one of the best law enforcement tools that officials have seen in 30 years."

Even so, fighting fingerprinting has become as much a litmus test of Southern-style political correctness as, say, battling gun control or opposing methods of identifying explosives.

In the war on fingerprints, the lions have made allies with the lambs. Very conservative legislators (Rep. Mitchell Kaye, Rep. Brian Joyce, Sen. Pam Glanton, etc.) have joined forces with the liberal American Civil Liberties Union to try to stop fingerprinting.

The campaign against imaging fingertips is not limited to members of the political fringes. Moderately conservative lawmakers, such as House Republican Leader Bob Irvin, Rep. Roy Barnes, and Rep. Terry Coleman, have signed measures to halt fingerprinting.

House Majority Leader Larry Walker has successfully led a campaign to restrict use of fingerprints and to limit the number of law enforcement agencies with access to them.

Rhetoric against fingerprinting sounds like lines from World War II propaganda movies. We are warned of the Gestapo breaking down our doors in the middle of the night to take us away. Or Nazi SS men, their

169

jack-boots slapping against cobblestones, going from house to house, matching fingerprints with dissidents.

This is simply nuts or plainly paranoid. The Department of Public Safety proposed fingerprinting as a way to control the increasing problem of drivers-license fraud.

Col. Miles said he thought he might be doing law-abiding Georgians a favor by requiring fingerprints as a way to protect their drivers license. In January, he wrote members of the General Assembly in defense of the proposal:

"The drivers license as official identification is used in every bank transaction from check cashing, credit card application, and applying for a loan. The drivers license is accepted as ID by airlines, all government agencies, retail, and wholesale establishments from grocery stores to car dealers, and many others. Most Georgians will probably show their license several times a week while making these transactions. I cannot express to you how important it is for us to maintain the accuracy and integrity of our Georgia drivers license."

Using a digital system of fingerprinting, Miles says, "will eliminate the possibility of a criminal obtaining a license under an innocent driver's name. It also will prohibit people from obtaining multiple licenses."

Most banking and retail-sales groups support the fingerprints. Polls show most Georgians favor fingerprinting to help collar criminals.

But the Georgia Legislature apparently has so little to do that some of its leading lights are expending much of their energy trying to rescue drivers from the ordeal of fingerprinting.

If you need an outlet for outrage, Pam, Mitchell, and Brian, there are many more suitable targets than a time-worn method of trying to secure driving permits and check-cashing ID.

Try railing against the night-stalking bombers who set off explosives in Atlanta. Or the doctors who are accused of stealing millions in research funds from the University System. Or corrupt politicians who swapped greenbacks for votes in the last election.

These alleged bad guys and dirty deeds deserve legislative attention. Come to think of it, a fingerprint at the right time and place might have stopped one or two of these culprits in their tracks.

INDEX

Published by Mercer University Press
October 1997

Book design by Marc A. Jolley.
Camera-ready pages composed on a Macintosh
    Performa 6300CD, via Microsoft Word 6.0.1.
Text font: Book Antiqua 10/12.
Printed and bound by McNaughton & Gunn, Inc.,
    Saline, Michigan.
Cased, smyth-sewn, and printed on acid-free paper.